Lecture Notes in Computer Scie

Edited by G. Goos, J. Hartmanis and J. van

Springer
Berlin
Heidelberg
New York
Barcelona
Hong Kong
London
Milan
Paris
Singapore
Tokyo

Frank Mueller (Ed.)

High-Level Parallel Programming Models and Supportive Environments

6th International Workshop, HIPS 2001
San Francisco, CA, USA, April 23, 2001
Proceedings

 Springer

Series Editors

Gerhard Goos, Karlsruhe University, Germany
Juris Hartmanis, Cornell University, NY, USA
Jan van Leeuwen, Utrecht University, The Netherlands

Volume Editor

Frank Mueller
Center for Applied Scientific Computing
Lawrence Livermore National Laboratory
P.O. Box 808, L-561, Livermore, CA 94551, USA
E-mail: frank.mueller@llnl.gov

Cataloging-in-Publication Data applied for

Die Deutsche Bibliothek - CIP-Einheitsaufnahme

High level parallel programming models and supportive environments :
6th international workshop / HIPS 2001, San Francisco, CA, USA, April
23, 2001. Frank Mueller (ed.). - Berlin ; Heidelberg ; New York ;
Barcelona ; Hong Kong ; London ; Milan ; Paris ; Singapore ; Tokyo :
Springer, 2001
  (Lecture notes in computer science ; Vol. 2026)
  ISBN 3-540-41944-6

CR Subject Classification (1998): D.1.3, D.3, D.4, D.2, F.2.1, F.3, C.2.4

ISSN 0302-9743
ISBN 3-540-41944-6 Springer-Verlag Berlin Heidelberg New York

Springer-Verlag Berlin Heidelberg New York
a member of BertelsmannSpringer Science+Business Media GmbH

http://www.springer.de

© Springer-Verlag Berlin Heidelberg 2001
Printed in Germany

Typesetting: Camera-ready by author
Printed on acid-free paper   SPIN: 10782395   06/3142   5 4 3 2 1 0

Preface

On the 23rd of April, 2001, the 6th Workshop on High-Level Parallel Programming Models and Supportive Environments (HIPS 2001) was held in San Francisco. HIPS has been held over the past six years in conjunction with IPDPS, the International Parallel and Distributed Processing Symposium.

The HIPS workshop focuses on the high-level programming of networks of workstations, computing clusters, and of massively-parallel machines. Its goal is to bring together researchers working in the areas of applications, language design, compilers, system architecture, and programming tools to discuss new developments in programming such systems.

In recent years, several standards have emerged with an increasing demand for support for parallel and distributed processing. On one hand, message-passing frameworks, such as PVM, MPI, and VIA, provide support for basic communication. On the other hand, distributed object standards, such as CORBA and DCOM, provide support for handling remote objects in a client-server fashion but also ensure certain guarantees for the quality of services.

The key issues for the success of programming parallel and distributed environments are high-level programming concepts and efficiency. In addition, other quality categories have to be taken into account, such as scalability, security, bandwidth guarantees, and fault tolerance, just to name a few.

Today's challenge is to provide high-level programming concepts without sacrificing efficiency. This can only be achieved by carefully designing for those concepts and by providing supportive programming environments that facilitate program development and tuning.

Past results in parallel computing on one side and distributed systems on the other side present opportunities for an increased transfer of knowledge between the areas. In particular, cluster computing presents a promising framework for parallel computing where advances from distributed systems can be utilized. Achievements in the area of automated performance analysis and performance modeling for parallel systems, on the other hand, may contribute to advances in performance analysis of distributed systems.

Future directions also include alternatives to current standardization practices, for example, by replacing client-server protocols with decentralized ones that may be more suitable for distributed systems. In addition, successful programming models, such as the shared-memory paradigm, should be investigated for new trends like cluster computing.

This workshop provides a forum for researchers and commercial developers to meet and discuss the various hardware and software issues involved in the design and use of high-level programming models and supportive environments.

HIPS 2001 featured an invited talk and presentations of ten refereed papers. The papers were selected out of 20 submissions. Twenty-one referees prepared multiple reviews for each submission. The recommendations of the referees determined an initial set of papers selected for acceptance. The members of the program committee were then given the task of resolving differences in opinion for the papers they refereed based on the written reviews. After the resolution process, the 10 papers included in the workshop proceedings were selected for presentation and publication. The papers cover the topics of:

- Concepts and languages for high-level parallel programming

- Concurrent object-oriented programming

- Distributed objects and components

- Structured parallel programming (skeletons, patterns, etc.)

- Software engineering principles for parallel systems

- Automatic parallelization and optimization

- High-level programming environments

- Automated performance analysis and performance modeling

- Debugging techniques and development tools

- Distributed shared memory

- Implementation techniques for high-level programming models

- Operating system support for runtime systems and middleware

- Architectural support for high-level programming models

- Guarantees for Quality of Service in distributed environments

- Security of communication for distributed execution

- Fault tolerance in network computing

Steering Committee

- Michael Gerndt, Forschungszentrum Jülich, Germany

- Hermann Hellwagner, Universität Klagenfurt, Austria

- Frank Mueller, Lawrence Livermore National Laboratory, USA

- Martin Schulz, Technische Universität München, Germany

Program Committee

- Henri Bal, Vrije Universiteit, The Netherlands
- Arndt Bode, Technische Universität München, Germany
- Luc Bougé, ENS Lyon, France
- Helmar Burkhart, Universität Basel, Switzerland
- John Carter, University of Utah, USA
- Karsten Decker, ETH Zürich, Switzerland
- Michael Gerndt, Forschungszentrum Jülich, Germany
- Hermann Hellwagner, Universität Klagenfurt, Austria
- Francois Irigoin, Ecole des Mines de Paris, France
- Vijay Karamcheti, New York University, USA
- Peter Keleher, University of Maryland, USA
- Gabriele Keller, University of Technology, Sydney, Australia
- Piyush Mehrotra, ICASE / NASA Lanley Research Center, USA
- Frank Mueller, Lawrence Livermore National Laboratory, USA
- Susanna Pelagatti, Università di Pisa, Italy
- Thierry Priol, IRISA, France
- Alexander Reinefeld, ZIB, Germany
- Martin Schulz, Technische Universität München, Germany
- Xian-He Sun, Illinois Institute of Technology, USA
- Domenico Talia, ISI-CNR, Italy
- George Thiruvathukal, DePaul University, USA

External Reviewers

- F. Bodin	- R. Wismüller	- W. Smith	- R. Perego
- J. Simon	- S. Rathmayer	- Y. JEGOU	- A. Zavanella
- F. Schintke	- Silber	- K. Chanchio	
- C. Perez	- R. Hood	- W. Karl	- M. Aldinucci

Acknowledgments

The workshop chair would like to acknowledge the following people:

- the invited speaker for his voluntary contributions to the workshop;

- the steering committee for their support during the planning phase;

- Richard Gerber for making the START software available to assist the submission and review process;

- Alfred Hofmann for his work as a contact person to Springer LNCS;

- and last but not least the eager members of the program committee and the external reviewers.

April 2001   Frank Mueller

[1]This work was performed under the auspices of the U.S. Department of Energy by the University of California, Lawrence Livermore National Laboratory under Contract No. W-7405-Eng-48.

Table of Contents

High-Level Data Mapping for Clusters of SMPs 1
Siegfried Benkner and Thomas Brandes

Integrating Task and Data Parallelism by Means of Coordination Patterns 16
Manuel Díaz, Bartolomé Rubio, Enrique Soler and José M. Troya

Using Loop-Level Parallelism to Parallelize Vectorizable Programs 28
D. M. Pressel, J. Sahu and K. R. Heavey

A Generic C++ Framework for Parallel Mesh-Based Scientific Applications . . . 45
Jens Gerlach, Peter Gottschling and Uwe Der

DSM-PM2: A Portable Implementation Platform for Multithreaded
DSM Consistency Protocols 55
Gabriel Antoniu and Luc Bougé

Implementation of a Skeleton-Based Parallel Programming Environment
Supporting Arbitrary Nesting 71
Rémi Coudarcher, Jocelyn Sérot and Jean-Pierre Dérutin

Supporting Soft Real-Time Tasks and QoS on the Java Platform 86
James C. Pang, Gholamali C. Shoja and Eric G. Manning

Evaluating the XMT Parallel Programming Model 95
Dorit Naishlos, Joseph Nuzman, Chau-Wen Tseng and Uzi Vishkin

DEPICT: A Topology-Based Debugger for MPI Programs 109
Simon Huband and Chris McDonald

Correcting Errors in Message Passing Systems 122
Jan B. Pedersen and Alan Wagner

High-Level Data Mapping for Clusters of SMPs[*]

Siegfried Benkner[1] and Thomas Brandes[2]

[1] Institute for Software Science
University of Vienna, Liechtensteinstr. 22, A-1090 Vienna, Austria
sigi@ieee.org

[2] SCAI - Institute for Algorithms and Scientific Computing
GMD - German National Research Center for Information Technology
Schloß Birlinghoven, D-53754 St. Augustin, Germany
brandes@gmd.de

Abstract. Clusters of shared-memory multiprocessors (SMPs) have become the most promising parallel computing platforms for scientific computing. However, SMP clusters significantly increase the complexity of user application development when using the low-level application programming interfaces MPI and OpenMP, forcing users to deal with both distributed-memory and shared-memory parallelization details. In this paper we present extensions of High Performance Fortran for SMP clusters which enable the compiler to adopt a hybrid parallelization strategy, efficiently combining distributed-memory with shared-memory parallelism. By means of a small set of new language features, the hierarchical structure of SMP clusters may be specified. This information is utilized by the compiler to derive inter-node data mappings for controlling distributed-memory parallelization across the nodes of a cluster, and intra-node data mappings for extracting shared-memory parallelism within nodes. Additional mechanisms are proposed for specifying inter- and intra-node data mappings explicitly, for controlling specific SM parallelization issues, and for integrating OpenMP routines in HPF applications. The proposed features are being realized within the ADAPTOR and VFC compiler. The parallelization strategy for clusters of SMPs adopted by these compilers is discussed as well as a hybrid-parallel execution model based on a combination of MPI and OpenMP. Early experimental results indicate the effectiveness of the proposed features.

Keywords: parallel programming, HPF, OpenMP, MPI, SMP clusters, parallelization, hybrid parallelism.

1 Introduction

Many supercomputer centers have introduced clusters of shared-memory multiprocessors (SMPs) as their premier high performance computing platforms. Examples of such systems are multiprocessor clusters from SUN, SGI, IBM, a variety of multi-processor PC clusters, supercomputers like the NEC SX-5 or the future Japanese Earth Simulator and the ASCI White machine.

[*] This work was supported by NEC Europe Ltd. as part of the ADVICE and AD-

Clusters of SMP systems increase the complexity of user applications development by forcing programmers to deal with shared-memory programming issues such as multi-threading and synchronization, as well as with distributed-memory issues such as data distribution and explicit message-passing.

There are mainly two trends in parallel programming, depending on how the address space of parallel systems is organized. On the one hand, the standard application programming interface (API) for message-passing, MPI [13], is widely used, mainly for distributed-memory systems. Recently, a standard API for shared-memory parallel programming, OpenMP [17], has become available. While OpenMP is restricted to shared-memory architectures only, MPI programs can also be executed on shared-memory machines and clusters.

However, MPI programs which are executed on clusters of SMPs usually do not directly utilize the shared-memory available within nodes and thus may miss a number of optimization opportunities. A promising approach for parallel programming attempts to combine MPI and OpenMP in a single application. Such a strategy attempts to fully exploit the potential of SMP clusters by relying on data distribution and explicit message-passing between the nodes of a cluster, and on shared-memory and multi-threading within the nodes. While such an approach allows optimizing parallel programs by taking the hybrid architecture of SMP clusters into account, applications written in such a way tend to become extremely complex.

In contrast to MPI and OpenMP, High Performance Fortran (HPF) is a high-level parallel programming language which can be employed on both distributed-memory and shared-memory machines. The data mapping provides the necessary data locality to minimize communication and synchronization that is generated automatically by the compiler. Although HPF programs can be compiled for clusters of SMPs, the language does not provide features for exploiting the hierarchical structure of clusters. As a consequence, current HPF compilers usually ignore the shared-memory aspect of SMP clusters and treat such machines as pure distributed-memory systems.

In order to overcome these shortcomings of HPF and its compilers, we propose extensions of the HPF mapping mechanisms such that the hierarchical structure of SMP clusters can be taken into account. Based on these features, an HPF compiler can then adopt a hybrid parallelization strategy whereby distributed-memory parallelism based on message-passing, e.g. MPI, is exploited across the nodes of a cluster, while shared-memory parallelism is exploited within SMP nodes by relying on multi-threading, e.g. OpenMP.

Two sets of HPF extensions for clusters of SMPs are proposed in this paper. The first set of extensions is based on the concept of *processor mappings*, a simple mechanism for specifying the hierarchical structure of SMP clusters by introducing *abstract node arrays* onto which abstract processor arrays may be mapped by means of the basic HPF distribution mechanisms. The second set of extensions allows the specification of *hierarchical data mappings* in two separate steps, comprising an *inter-node data mapping* which maps data arrays onto abstract node arrays and an *intra-node data mapping* which maps node-local data onto processors within a node. Additional language mechanisms are provided for the integration of OpenMP routines or other node routines that operate only on data local to a node.

The rest of this paper is organized as follows. Section 2 proposes language features for optimizing existing HPF programs for clusters of SMPs by providing an explicit specification of the hierarchical structure of clusters. Section 3 sketches a hierarchical compilation and execution model for clusters of SMPs which is adopted for the parallelization of HPF programs that utilize the proposed language extensions. Section 4 describes a set of additional HPF extensions for specifying inter-node and intra-node data mappings explicitly, and a new EXTRINSIC model for integrating OpenMP routines into HPF applications. Related work is discussed in Section 5. Finally, conclusions and a discussion of future work are presented in Section 6.

2   Exploiting the Hierarchical Structure of SMP Clusters

HPF provides the concept of abstract processor arrangements to establish an abstraction of the underlying parallel target architecture in the form of one or more rectilinear processor arrays. Processor arrays are utilized within data distribution directives to describe a mapping of array elements to abstract processors. Array elements mapped to an abstract processor are *owned* by that processor. *Ownership* of data is the central concept for the execution of data parallel programs. Based on the ownership of data, the distribution of computations to abstract processors and the necessary communication and synchronization are derived automatically.

Consider now an SMP cluster consisting of NN nodes, each equipped with NPN processors. Currently, if an HPF program is targeted to an SMP cluster, abstract processors are either associated with the NN nodes of the cluster or with the $NN * NPN$ processors. In the first case, data arrays are distributed only across the NN nodes of the cluster and therefore only parallelism of degree NN can be exploited. In the second case, where abstract HPF processors are associated with all processors available in the cluster, potential parallelism of degree $NN * NPN$ can be exploited. However, by viewing an SMP cluster as a distributed-memory machine consisting of $NN * NPN$ processors, the shared-memory available within nodes is usually not exploited, since data distribution and communication are performed within nodes as well.

In the following we propose language features for optimizing existing HPF programs for clusters of SMPs by providing an explicit specification of the hierarchical structure of clusters.

2.1   Processor Mappings

The concept of *processor mappings* is introduced in order to describe the hierarchical structure of SMP clusters. A processor mapping specifies a mapping of an abstract processor array to an abstract node array. The NODES *directive* is introduced for declaring one or more abstract node arrays. For the specification of processor mappings a subset of the HPF data distribution mechanisms as provided by the DISTRIBUTE directive are utilized.

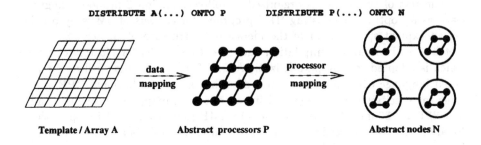

Fig. 1. Processor mappings. The hierarchical structure of SMP clusters is described by mapping processor arrays to node arrays using a subset of HPF's distribution mechanisms.

As a consequence of a processor mapping, each processor of an abstract processor array is mapped to a node of an abstract node array. Processor mappings are specified by using a subset of the HPF distribution mechanisms. For homogeneous clusters, the usual HPF BLOCK distribution format may be used. Heterogeneous clusters can be supported by means of the GEN_BLOCK distribution format of the Approved Extensions of HPF.

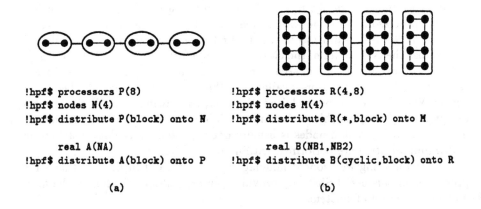

```
!hpf$ processors P(8)
!hpf$ nodes N(4)
!hpf$ distribute P(block) onto N

      real A(NA)
!hpf$ distribute A(block) onto P

            (a)
```

```
!hpf$ processors R(4,8)
!hpf$ nodes M(4)
!hpf$ distribute R(*,block) onto M

      real B(NB1,NB2)
!hpf$ distribute B(cyclic,block) onto R

            (b)
```

Fig. 2. Examples of processor mappings. On the left-hand side Figure (a) shows a 4x2 SMP cluster, while on the right-hand side Figure (b) illustrates a cluster of 4 nodes each with 8 processors, arranged in a 4x2 configuration.

Figure 1 illustrates the concept of processor mappings while examples of processor mappings are shown in Figures 2 and 3. Figure 2 (a) shows how the hierarchical structure of an SMP cluster, consisting of 4 nodes with 2 processors each, may be specified. Figure 2 (b) specifies an SMP cluster, consisting of 4 nodes with 8 processors each, where the processors within a node are arranged as a 4x2 array. Figure 3 specifies a heterogeneous SMP cluster, consisting of 4 nodes with 2, 3, 4, and 3 processors, respectively. Here the GEN_BLOCK distribution format of HPF is utilized to indicate that the number of processors within nodes varies.

```
      integer, dimension(4):: SIZE = (/2,3,4,3/)
!hpf$ processors R(12)
!hpf$ nodes M(4)
!hpf$ distribute R(gen_block(SIZE)) onto M
```

Fig. 3. A heterogeneous SMP cluster with four nodes. The GEN_BLOCK distribution format is used to specify the number of processors available in each node.

In order to support abstract node arrays whose sizes are determined upon start of a program, the new intrinsic function NUMBER_OF_NODES is provided. NUMBER_OF_NODES returns the actual number of nodes used to execute a program in the same way as the HPF intrinsic function NUMBER_OF_PROCESSORS returns the total number of processors used to execute an HPF program.

Processor mappings provide a simple means for optimizing HPF applications for SMP clusters. Using processor mappings, the hierarchical structure of SMP clusters may be specified explicitly, without the need to change existing HPF directives. Based on a processor mapping, an HPF compiler can adopt a cluster-specific parallelization strategy in order to exploit distributed-memory parallelism across the nodes of a cluster, and shared-memory parallelism within nodes.

2.2 Exploiting DM and SM Parallelism

If a dimension of an abstract processor array is distributed by the format BLOCK or GEN_BLOCK, contiguous blocks of processors are mapped to the nodes in the corresponding dimension of the specified abstract node array. As a consequence of such a processor mapping, both distributed-memory parallelism and shared-memory parallelism may be exploited for all data array dimensions that are mapped to that processor array dimension. On the other hand, if in a processor mapping a dimension of an abstract processor array is distributed by means of "*", all abstract processors in that dimension are mapped to the same node of an abstract node array, and thus only shared-memory parallelism may be exploited across array dimensions which have been mapped to that processor array dimension.

In the first example (Figure 2 (a)), both distributed- and shared-memory parallelism may be exploited for array A. In the other example (Figure 2 (b)), only shared-memory parallelism may be exploited across the first dimension of array B, while both shared-memory and distributed-memory parallelism may be exploited across the second dimension of B.

2.3 Deriving Inter- and Intra-Node Mappings

An HPF data mapping directive, e.g. DISTRIBUTE A(BLOCK) ONTO P, determines for each processor P(I) of the abstract processor array P those parts of the data array A that are owned by P(I). If, in addition, a processor mapping for P with respect to a node array N is specified, an inter-node data mapping may be automatically derived from the data mapping and the processor mapping.

An *inter-node data mapping* determines for each node N(J) those parts of array A that are owned by node N(J). The implicit assumption is that those portions of an array owned by a node are allocated in an unpartitioned way in the shared memory of this node, while data is distributed across the local memory of nodes, according to inter-node mapping.

In the same way, an *intra-node data mapping* may be derived from a data mapping and a processor mapping. Intra-node data mappings specify a mapping of the data allocated on a node of a cluster with respect to the processors within a node. Here, we assume that intra-node data mappings are utilized by the compiler to control the exploitation of shared-memory parallelism within SMP nodes. This is described in more detail in the next section.

3 Compilation and Execution Model

In this section we briefly sketch a hierarchical compilation and execution model for clusters of SMPs which is adopted for the parallelization of HPF programs that utilize the proposed language extensions. This model is currently being realized within the ADAPTOR HPF compilation system [4] and within the VFC [1] compiler.

3.1 Outline of the Compilation Strategy

Both the ADAPTOR and the VFC compiler are source-to-source translation systems which transform an HPF program into an explicitly parallel Fortran program which is then compiled by the Fortran compiler of the parallel target machine in order to obtain an executable parallel program. As opposed to the usual HPF compilation, where a single-threaded SPMD node program is generated, a multi-threaded node program is generated under the hierarchical execution model.

An extended HPF program is compiled in two phases for clusters of SMPs. In the first compilation phase the compiler analyzes the data mappings and processor mappings in order to determine an inter-node data mapping. Based on the inter-node data mapping, the compiler distributes data and work across nodes and inserts message-passing primitives in order to realize the communication of non-local data between the nodes of a cluster. The result of the first compilation phase is an SPMD Fortran/MPI message-passing program.

In Figure 4 (b) the first compilation phase is illustrated for a simple HPF code fragment showing a reduction operation on a two-dimensional array. Due to the specified processor mapping, the first dimension of B is classified as **shared** while the second dimension is classified as **distributed**. As a consequence, the second dimension of B is distributed across the 4 nodes, while the first dimension is not distributed. The **SUM** intrinsic function is transformed into a nested loop. The outer loop is strip-mined across the nodes of the cluster. The call to HPFrt_DM_get_my_bounds ensures that each node operates only on its local part of B. After the loop, communication bewteen nodes is performed by means of mpi_allreduce in order to combine the partial results of all nodes.

In the second phase the intermediate SPMD program is parallelized for shared-memory according to the intra-node data mapping derived by the compiler. Shared-memory parallelization is currently realized by inserting corresponding OpenMP directives in order to distribute the work of a node among multiple threads. Work distribution of loops and array assignments is derived from the intra-node data mapping of the accessed arrays and realized by corresponding OpenMP work-sharing constructs and/or appropriate loop transformations (e.g. strip-mining). Similarly, data consistency of shared data objects is enforced by inserting appropriate OpenMP synchronization primitives.

As shown in Figure 4 (c) during the second compilation phase the SPMD message-passing program is transformed by inserting OpenMP directives in order to exploit shared-memory parallelism within the nodes of the cluster. The OpenMP **parallel** directive ensures that multiple threads are generated on each node, and the call to HPFrt_SM_get_my_bounds enforces that each thread executes its own chunk of inner loop iterations.

3.2 The Hierarchical Execution Model

HPF programs compiled for clusters of SMPs as outlined above, are executed according to a *hierarchical execution model*. Within the hierarchical execution model an HPF program is executed by a set of parallel processes, each of which executes on a separate node of an SMP cluster within its own local address space. Usually, every abstract HPF node is associated with a separate MPI-process executed on a single node of the cluster. Process parallelism, data partitioning, and message-passing communication based on MPI is utilized across nodes.

Each node process generates a set of threads which emulate the abstract processors mapped to a node and which execute concurrently in the shared address space of a node. The data mapped to one node is allocated in a non-partitioned way in the shared memory, regardless of the intra-node mapping. Parallel execution of threads within nodes is organized on the basis of the derived intra-node data mapping which controls the distribution of computations among the threads. Consistency of shared data objects is guaranteed by automatically generated synchronization primitives [2].

```
!hpf$ processors P(6,4)
!hpf$ nodes N(4)
!hpf$ distribute P(*, block) onto N
      real B(NB1,NB2), S
!hpf$ distribute B(block, block) onto P
      ...
      S = sum(B)
```

(a) Original HPF program

```
      real B(NB1,NB2/4), S    ! for simplicity: NB2 is a multiple of 4
      integer B_DSP (...)     ! internal array descriptor for B
      integer B_LB2, B_UB2
      ...                     ! build array descriptor
      S = 0.0
      call HPFrt_DM_get_my_bounds (B_DSP, 2, B_LB2, B_UB2)
      do I = B_LB2, B_UB2
         do J = 1, NB1
            S = S + B(J,I)
         end do
      end do
      call mpi_allreduce (S, S, 1, MPI_REAL, MPI_SUM, MPI_COMM_WORLD, IERR)
```

(b) Phase 1: Intermediate SPMD Fortran/MPI message-passing node program.

```
      ...
      integer B_LB1, B_UB1, B_LB2, B_UB2
      ...                                 ! build array descriptor
      S = 0.0
      call HPFrt_DM_get_my_bounds (B_DSP, 2, B_LB2, B_UB2)
!$omp parallel, private (I,J,B_LB1,B_UB1), reduction(S)
      call HPFrt_SM_get_my_bounds (B_DSP, 1, B_LB1, B_UB1)
      do I = B_LB2, B_UB2
         do J = B_LB1, B_UB1
            S = S + B(J,I)
         end do
      end do
!$omp end parallel
      call mpi_allreduce (S, S, 1, MPI_REAL, MPI_SUM, MPI_COMM_WORLD, IERR)
```

(c) Phase 2: Generated hybrid-parallel MPI/OpenMP program.

Fig. 4. Compilation of a HPF program for clusters of SMPs.

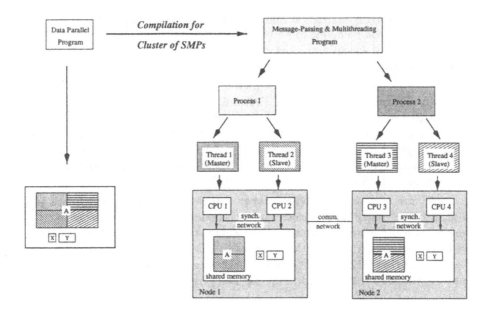

Fig. 5. Hierarchical HPF execution model.

3.3 Experiments

In this section we report on early experiments with the proposed language extensions and the hierarchical compilation and execution model on a dual-processor PC cluster. For the performance experiments, we used an existing HPF kernel from a numerical pricing module [14] developed in the context of the AURORA Financial Management System [7]. This kernel realizes a backward induction algorithm on a Hull and White interest rate tree. In the HPF code the interest rate tree is represented by 2-dimensional arrays and several index vectors which capture the structure of the tree. All these arrays have been distributed by usual HPF distribution mechanisms. The main computations are performed in an inner **INDEPENDENT** loop with indirect data accesses, which operates on a single level of the Hull and White tree. Due to the peculiarities of the algorithm, communication is required for each level of the tree, introducing a significant communication overhead.

For the performance experiments, we computed the price of a variable coupon bond with a maturity of 10 years on a one-day basis, resulting in a tree with 3650 levels. We compared the original HPF kernel to an extended kernel, where an additional processor mapping was used for specifying the hierarchical structure of the PC cluster. Both kernels have been parallelized with the VFC compiler [1] and executed on a Beowulf cluster consisting of 8 nodes, each equipped with two Pentium II (400MHz) processors, connected by Fast Ethernet. The pgf90 compiler from Portland Group Inc. was used as a back-end compiler of VFC for compiling the generated MPI/OpenMP program.

The original HPF kernel was compiled by VFC to Fortran/MPI, while the extended kernel was compiled to Fortran/MPI/OpenMP and executed according to the hierarchical execution model utilizing MPI process parallelism across the nodes of the cluster and OpenMP thread parallelism within nodes.

The original HPF kernel has been measured in two different ways which are labeled in Figure 6 HPF/MPI-P and HPF/MPI-N, respectively. HPF/MPI-P refers to the MPI code generated by VFC and executed on 2 to 16 processors, where both processors were utilized on each node. HPF/MPI-N refers to the MPI version of the generated code executed on 2 to 8 nodes, where only one processor was utilized on each node. HPF-Cluster/MPI-OpenMP refers to the hybrid parallel code generated by VFC from the extended HPF kernel.

As Figure 6 shows, the HPF-Cluster kernel significantly outperforms the original HPF kernel, if both processors in a node are used. One reason for this performance difference seems to be the communication overhead induced by MPI communication[1] within the nodes of the cluster. The times measured for the HPF-Cluster/MPI-OpenMP and HPF/MPI-N variants were almost the same, however, the HPF/MPI-N version required twice as many nodes.

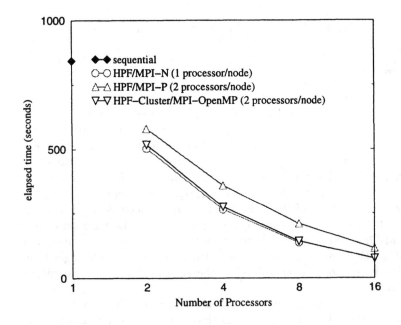

Fig. 6. Experimental Results

---

[1] The MPI version used on the PC cluster did not offer an optimized intra-node communication via shmem.

4 Additional Language Features

As outlined in the previous section, the introduction of abstract node arrays and processor mappings allows the specification of the hierarchical structure of SMP clusters. Based on these features, an HPF compiler may derive from existing HPF distribution an inter-node mapping which is utilized to distribute data across the nodes of a cluster, and an intra-node mapping in order to exploit shared-memory parallelism within nodes.

In this Section we describe a set of additional HPF extensions which to enable programmers to specify inter-node data mappings and intra-node data mappings explicitly. Such mappings are referred to as *hierarchical data mappings* and are defined in two steps. First, arrays are distributed to the nodes of a cluster, and second, node-local data is mapped to the processors within a cluster.

4.1 Hierarchical Data Mappings

A hierarchical data mapping may be specified explicitly by the user by first mapping data arrays onto abstract node arrays, and then specifying a mapping of node-local data with respect to the processors within a node. The first mapping is referred to as an *explicit inter-node data mapping*, and the second mapping is called *explicit intra-node data mapping*.

Inter-node data mappings may be specified explicitly by means of the HPF DISTRIBUTE directive which has been extended such that data arrays may be distributed directly onto abstract node arrays. The semantics of a distribution directive with an abstract nodes array as *distribution target* is equivalent to the semantics of a usual HPF distribution directive, except that data is now distributed only with respect to the nodes of a cluster. Processors within a node of a cluster usually have access to all data mapped to the shared memory of a node.

In addition to an inter-node mapping, an intra-node mapping may be explicitly specified by means of the SHARE directive. An intra-node data mapping specifies a mapping of node-local data to the abstract processors (threads) within a node. The syntax of the SHARE directive is similar to the DISTRIBUTE directive, but does not include an ONTO clause. The target of the mapping is the set of abstract processors available within a node.

The SHARE directive is used to control the distribution of work among the threads available on a node. In this context, the OpenMP work-sharing formats DYNAMIC and GUIDED may be employed in addition to the usual HPF distribution formats BLOCK, CYCLIC, and GEN_BLOCK.

4.2 Controlling the Work Sharing of Loops

An inter-node mapping explicitly specified by a SHARE directive for certain arrays is utilized in order to determine the work sharing of parallel loops or array assignments where such arrays are accessed. The user may override such an automatic strategy by appending a SHARE clause to an INDEPENDENT directive.

```
!hpf$ nodes N(8)
      real A(1000,1000)
!hpf$ distribute A(block,*) onto N !inter-node mapping (data distribution)
!hpf$ share A(*,block)              !intra-node mapping (work sharing)

...
!hpf$ independent, share(dynamic)
      do J = 1, N
         A(:,J) = f (A(:,J))
      end do
```

Fig. 7. Hierarchical data mappings. The first dimension of **A** is distributed by **block** onto the nodes of an SMP cluster, while for the second dimension of **A** a **block** work sharing strategy is specified by means of the **share** directive. Note that the work sharing information provided for an array in the specification part of a program may be overwritten at individual loops by attaching a **share** clause to an **independent** directive.

An example of a hierarchical mapping is shown in Figure 7. Assuming a homogeneous cluster of 8 nodes, each of which equipped with NPN processors, the inter-node mapping specified by means of the DISTRIBUTE directive distributes the first dimension of array A across the 8 nodes of the cluster, mapping a sub-array of shape (125,1000) to each node. The SHARE directive specifies a virtual distribution within each node. As a consequence, a sub-array of shape (125,1000/NPN) is mapped to each processor within a node. The SHARE clause attached to the INDEPENDENT directive specifies that a dynamic scheduling strategy should be adopted for scheduling the loop iterations of the J-loop among the threads executing on the processors within nodes. Without the SHARE clause a BLOCK-scheduling strategy would be adopted according to the specified intra-node mapping.

4.3   Integration of OpenMP Routines

The LOCAL extrinsic model of HPF [10] provides the possibility to write code that is executed on all active processors, where each processor has direct access only to its local data. We introduce a new extrinsic model, called NODE_LOCAL, that allows writing code which is executed on all active nodes, where on each node only node-local data according to the inter-node mapping is directly accessible. In NODE_LOCAL routines the potential shared-memory parallelism within nodes can be exploited independently of the HPF level.

A NODE_LOCAL subprogram can be written in one of the following languages:

- 'HPF', referring to the HPF language, where the HPF compiler can take advantage of the fact that only processors on the same node are involved.
- 'FORTRAN', referring to the ANSI/ISO standard Fortran language, in which the user can take advantage of thread parallelism, for example, via OpenMP.

```
extrinsic (MODEL=NODE_LOCAL) subroutine Sub(A)
   real, dimension :: A(:,:)
   integer N

!$OMP   parallel
        ...
end subroutine
```

Fig. 8. Example of a NODE_LOCAL EXTRINSIC routine.

Node-local HPF procedures can use any HPF intrinsic or library procedure. Similar to the HPF Local Routine Library, a new HPF Node Local Routine Library is provided for the use within HPF node-local routines, and a Fortran Node Local Routine Library which realizes the HPF Node Local Routines with a Fortran interface.

Node-local Fortran routines are very similar to local Fortran routines. The only difference is that the programmer now sees in the subprogram only the data mapped to a node instead of the data mapped to a processor. It is the programmers responsibility to exploit parallelism across multiple processors within a node, e.g. via OpenMP or via any other thread library.

5   Related Work

Several researchers have investigated the advantages of a hybrid programming model based on MPI and OpenMP against a unified MPI-only model. Cappelo [5] et al. investigated a hybrid-parallel programming strategy in comparison with a pure message passing approach using the NAS benchmarks on IBM SP systems. In their experiments the MPI-only approach is better than a hybrid strategy for most codes. They conclude that a hybrid-parallel strategy becomes superior when fast processors make the communication performance significant and the level of parallelization is sufficient. Henty [9] reports on experiments with a Discrete Element Modeling code on various SMP clusters. He concludes that current OpenMP implementations are not yet efficient enough for hybrid parallelism to outperform pure message-passing. Haan [8] performed experiments with a matrix-transpose showing that a hybrid-parallel approach can significantly outperform message-passing parallelization.

On the Origin2000, the SGI data placement directives [16] form a vendor specific extension of OpenMP. Some of these extensions have similar functionality as the HPF directives, e.g. "affinity scheduling" of parallel loops is the counterpart to the ON clause of HPF. Compaq has also added a new set of directives to its Fortran for Tru64 UNIX that extend the OpenMP Fortran API to control the placement of data in memory and the placement of computations that operate on that data [3].

Chapman, Mehrotra and Zima [6] propose a set of OpenMP extensions, similar to HPF mapping directives, for locality control, but they do not provide a execution model or implementation scheme.

Portland Group, Inc. proposes a high-level programming model [12] that extends the OpenMP API with additional data mapping directives, library routines and environment variables. This model extends OpenMP in order to control data locality with respect to the nodes of SMP clusters. In contrast to this model, HPF, with the extensions proposed in this paper, supports locality control across nodes as well as within nodes.

All these other approaches introduce data mapping features into OpenMP in order to increase locality, but still utilize the explicit work distribution via the PARALLEL and PARDO directives of OpenMP. Our approach is based on HPF and relies on an implicit work distribution which is usually derived from the data mapping but which may be explicitly controlled by the user within nodes by means of OpenMP-like extensions.

A number of researches have addressed the issues of implementing OpenMP on clusters of SMPs relying on a distributed-shared memory (DSM) software layer. Hu et al. [11] describe the implementation of OpenMP on a network of shared-memory multiprocessors by means of a translating OpenMP directives into calls to a modified version of the TreadMarks software distributed memory system. Sato et al. [15] describe the design of an OpenMP compiler for SMP clusters based on a compiler-directed DSM software layer.

6 Conclusions and Future Work

The concept of processor mappings enables HPF programmers to provide the compiler with an explicit description of the hierarchical structure of SMP clusters. The corresponding directives for the definition of abstract node arrays and the mapping of abstract processor arrays to abstract node arrays can also be considered as implementation-dependent directives that go conform with the current HPF language definition and therefore enable an easy way to port existing HPF programs to SMP clusters.

Additional extensions are provided for the explicit specification of inter-node and intra-node data mappings. These features give users more control over exploiting shared-memory parallelism within a node, by using the SHARE directive and SHARE clause, or the new NODE_LOCAL extrinsic model.

The directives, in either case, do not add significant complexity to the source code. Default processor arrays and node arrays in missing ONTO clauses can be chosen in such a way that many HPF programs do not need any modification at all. But the new extensions will be very helpful when the shared-memory parallelism is more advantageous than the distributed-memory parallelism for certain dimensions of the involved arrays.

A complete specification of the syntax and semantics of the proposed language extensions is subject of ongoing work. Major issues are the provision of data mapping mechanisms with respect to subsets of nodes as well as an integration of the new features with the HPF and/or OpenMP tasking model. Moreover, the evaluation of the new execution model in comparison with a pure message-passing model and the investigation of its relevance for a larger range of scientific applications will be addressed in future work.

References

1. S. Benkner. VFC: The Vienna Fortran Compiler. *Scientific Programming*, 7(1):67–81, 1999.

2. S. Benkner and T. Brandes. Exploiting Data Locality on Scalable Shared Memory Machines with Data Parallel Programs. In *Euro-Par 2000 Parallel Processing, Munich*, pages 647–657. Lecture Notes in Computer Science (1900), September 2000.

3. J. Bircsak, P. Craig, R. Crowell, Z. Cvetanovic, J. Harris, C. Nelson, and C. Offner. Extending OpenMP for NUMA Machines. In *Proceedings of SC 2000: High Performance Networking and Computing Conference*, Dallas, November 2000.

4. T. Brandes and F. Zimmermann. ADAPTOR - A Transformation Tool for HPF Programs. In K.M. Decker and R.M. Rehmann, editors, *Programming Environments for Massively Parallel Distributed Systems*, pages 91–96. Birkhäuser Verlag, April 1994.

5. F. Cappello and D. Etieble. MPI versus MPI+OpenMP on the IBM SP for the NAS Benchmarks. In *Proceedings of SC 2000: High Performance Networking and Computing Conference*, Dallas, November 2000.

6. B. Chapman, P. Mehrotra, and H. Zima. Enhancing OpenMP with Features for Locality Control. In *Proc. ECWMF Workshop "Towards Teracomputing - The Use of Parallel Processors in Meteorology"*, 1998.

7. E. Dockner, H. Moritsch, G. Ch. Pflug, and A. Swietanowski. AURORA financial management system: From Model Design to Implementation. Technical report AURORA TR1998-08, University of Vienna, June 1998.

8. O. Haan. Matrix Transpose with Hybrid OpenMP / MPI Parallelization. Technical Report Presentation given at SCICOMP 2000, http://www.spscicomp.org/2000/userpres.html#haan, 2000.

9. D. S. Henty. Performance of Hybrid Message-Passing and Shared-Memory Parallelism for Discrete Element Modeling. In *Proceedings of SC 2000: High Performance Networking and Computing Conference*, Dallas, November 2000.

10. High Performance Fortran Forum. High Performance Fortran Language Specification. Version 2.0, Department of Computer Science, Rice University, January 1997.

11. Y. Hu, H. Lu, A. Cox, and W. Zwaenepel. Openmp for networks of smps. In *Proceedings of IPPS.*, 1999.

12. M. Leair, J. Merlin, S. Nakamoto, V. Schuster, and M. Wolfe. Distributed OMP – A Programming Model for SMP Clusters. In *Eighth International Workshop on Compilers for Parallel Computers*, pages 229–238, Aussois, France, January 2000.

13. Message Passing Interface Forum. MPI: A Message-Passing Interface Standard. Vers. 1.1, June 1995. MPI-2: Extensions to the Message-Passing Interface, 1997.

14. H. Moritsch and S. Benkner. High Performance Numerical Pricing Methods. In *4-th Intl. HPF Users Group Meeting*, Tokyo, October 2000.

15. M. Sato, S. Satoh, K. Kusano, and Y. Tanaka. Design of openmp compiler for an smp cluster. In *Proceedings EWOMP '99, pp.32-39.*, 1999.

16. Silicon Graphics Inc. MIPSpro Power Fortran 77 Programmer's Guide: OpenMP Multiprocessing Directives. Technical Report Document 007-2361-007, 1999.

17. The OpenMP Forum. OpenMP Fortran Application Program Interface. Version 1.1, November 1999. http://www.openmp.org.

Integrating Task and Data Parallelism
by Means of Coordination Patterns*

Manuel Díaz, Bartolomé Rubio, Enrique Soler, and José M. Troya

Dpto. Lenguajes y Ciencias de la Computación. Málaga University
29071 Málaga, SPAIN
{mdr, tolo, esc, troya}@lcc.uma.es
http://www.lcc.uma.es

Abstract. This paper shows, by means of some examples, the suitability and expressiveness of a pattern-based approach to integrate task and data parallelism. Coordination skeletons or patterns express task parallelism among a collection of data parallel HPF tasks. Patterns specify the interaction among domains involved in the application along with the processor and data layouts. On the one hand, the use of domains, i.e. regions together with some interaction information, improves pattern reusability. On the other hand, the knowledge at the coordination level of data distribution belonging to the different HPF tasks is the key for an efficient implementation of the communication among them. Besides that, our system implementation requires no change to the runtime system support of the HPF compiler used. We also present some experimental results that show the efficiency of the model.

1 Introduction

High Performance Fortran (HPF) [13] has emerged as a standard data parallel, high level programming language for parallel computing. However, a disadvantage of using a parallel language like HPF is that the user is constrained by the model of parallelism supported by the language. It is widely accepted that many important parallel applications cannot be efficiently implemented following a pure data-parallel paradigm: pipelines of data parallel tasks [10], a common computation structure in image processing, signal processing or computer vision; multi-block codes containing irregularly structured regular meshes [1]; multidisciplinary optimization problems like aircraft design [5]. For these applications, rather than having a single data-parallel program, it is more appropriate to subdivide the whole computation into several data-parallel pieces, where these run concurrently and co-operate, thus exploiting task parallelism.

Integration of task and data parallelism is currently an active area of research and several approaches have been proposed [12][11][19]. Integrating the two forms of parallelism cleanly and within a coherent programming model is difficult [2]. In general, compiler-based approaches are limited in terms of the

---

* This work was supported by the Spanish project CICYT TIC-99-1083-C02-01

forms of task parallelism structures they can support, and runtime solutions require that the programmer have to manage task parallelism at a lower level than data parallelism. The use of coordination models and languages [4] and structured parallel programming [15] is proving to be a good alternative, providing high level mechanisms and supporting different forms of task parallelism structures in a clear and elegant way [16][6].

In [9] we presented DIP (Domain Interaction Patterns), a new approach of integrating task and data parallelism using skeletons. DIP is a high level coordination language to express task parallelism among a collection of data parallel HPF tasks, which interact according to static and predictable patterns. It allows an application to be organized as a combination of common skeletons, such as multi-blocking or pipelining. Skeletons specify the interaction among domains involved in the application along with the mapping of processors and data distribution.

On the one hand, the use of domains, which are regions together with some interaction information such as borders, make the language suitable for the solution of numerical problems, especially those with an irregular surface that can be decomposed into regular, block structured domains. In this paper, we prove how it can be successfully used on the solution of domain decomposition-based problems and multi-block codes. Moreover, we show how other kinds of problems with a communication pattern based on (sub)arrays interchange (2-D FFT, Convolution, Narrowband Tracking Radar, etc.) may be defined and solved in an easy and clear way. The use of domains also avoids that some computational aspects involved in the application, such as data types, have to appear at the coordination level, as it occurs in other approaches [16][6]. This improves pattern reusability.

On the other hand, the knowledge at the coordination level of data distribution belonging to the different HPF tasks is the key for an efficient implementation of the communication and synchronization among them. In DIP, unlike in other proposals [11][6], the inter-task communication schedule is established at compilation time. Moreover, our approach requires no change to the runtime support of the HPF compiler used. In this paper, we also present some implementation issues of a developed initial prototype and confirm the efficiency of the model by means of some experimental results.

The rest of the paper is structured as follows. Section 1.1 discusses related work. Section 2 gives an overview of DIP. In section 3, the expressiveness and suitability of the model to integrate task and data parallelism is demonstrated by means of some examples. Section 4 discusses the implementation issues and preliminary results and, finally, in section 5, some conclusions are sketched.

1.1 Related Work

In recent years, several proposals have addressed integration of task and data parallelism. We shall state a few of them and discuss the relative contributions of our approach.

The Fx model [19] expresses task parallelism by providing declaration directives to partition processors into subgroups and execution directives to assign computations to different subgroups (task regions). These task regions can be dynamically nested. The new standard HPF 2.0 [12] of the data parallel language HPF provides approved extensions for task parallelism, which allow nested task and data parallelism, following a similar model to that of Fx. These extensions allow the spawning of tasks but do not allow interaction like synchronization and communication between tasks during their execution and therefore might be too restrictive for certain application classes. Differently from these proposals, DIP does not need the adoption of new task parallel HPF constructs to express task parallelism. DIP is a coordination layer for HPF tasks which are separately compiled by an off-the-shelf HPF compiler that requires no change, while the task parallel coordination level is provided by the corresponding DIP library.

In HPF/MPI [11], the message-passing library MPI has been added to HPF. This definition of an HPF binding for MPI attempts to resolve the ambiguities appeared when a communication interface for sequential languages is invoked from a parallel one. In an HPF/MPI program, each task constitutes an independent HPF program in which one logical thread of control operates on arrays distributed across a statically defined set of processors. At the same time, each task is also one logical process in an MPI computation. In our opinion, the adoption of a message-passing paradigm to directly express HPF task parallelism is too low-level. Moreover, in our approach, the inter-task communication schedule is established at compilation time from the information provided at the coordination level related to the inter-domain connections and data distribution. In this case, expressiveness and good performance are our relative contributions.

Another coordination language for mixed task and data parallel programs has been proposed in [16]. The model provides a framework for the complete derivation process in which a specification program is transformed into a coordination program. The former expresses possible execution orders between modules and describes the available degree of task parallelism. The latter describes how the available degree of parallelism is actually exploited for a specific parallel implementation. The result is a complete description of a parallel program that can easily be translated into a message-passing program. This proposal is more a specification approach than a programming approach. The programmer is responsible for specifying the available task parallelism, but the final decision whether the available task parallelism will be exploited and how the processors should be partitioned into groups is taken by the compiler. Moreover, it is not based on HPF. The final message-passing program is expressed in C with MPI.

Possibly the closest proposal to DIP is taskHPF [6]. It is also a high level coordination language to define the interaction patterns among HPF tasks in a declarative way. Applications considered are also structured as ensembles of independent data parallel HPF modules, which interact according to static and predictable patterns. taskHPF provides a pipeline pattern and directives which help the programmer in balancing the pipelined stages: ON PROCESSORS directive fixes the number of processors assigned to an HPF task and REPLICATE directive can be used to replicate non-scalable stages. Patterns can be composed together to build complex structures in a declarative way. Our approach has also a pipeline pattern with similar directives. However, the differences are substancial: a) we work with domains, without considering data types at coordination level, which can improve pattern reusability; b) our pattern do not force the utilization of ending marks, such as END_OF_STREAM, in the computational part, i.e. inside an HPF task; c) our pattern provides information about the future data distribution together with the processor layout, which allows scheduling the inter-task communication pattern at compilation time. On the other hand, DIP provides a multi-block pattern that make the language suitable for the solution of domain decomposition-based problems and multi-block codes.

The implementation of taskHPF is based on $COLT_{HPF}$ [14], a runtime support specifically designed for the coordination of concurrent and communicating HPF tasks. It is implemented on top of MPI (there is a new version using PVM) and requires small changes to the runtime support of the HPF compiler used. DIP implementation is based on BCL [8], a Border-based Coordination Language focused on the solution of numerical problems, especially those with an irregular surface that can be decomposed into regular, block structured domains. BCL is also implemented on top of the MPI communication layer, but no change to the HPF compiler has been needed.

Finally, it is worthy of remark some others skeletal coordination approaches with goals quite different from those of DIP. In [7], Activity Graphs are defined to provide an intermediate layer for the process of skeletal program compilation, serving as a common, language independent target notation for the translation from purely skeletal code, and as the source notation for the specific phase of base language code generation. In the former role they also provide a precise operational semantics for the skeletal layer. In [18], it is described the way the Network Of Tasks model [17] is used to built programs. This model is a extremely powerful program composition technique which is both semantically clean and transparent about performance. Software developers can reliably predict the performance of their programs from the knowledge of the the performance of the component nodes and the visible graph structure.

2 The DIP Coordination Language

In this section we only give a brief summary of the DIP language. More detailed description of DIP appears in [9].

DIP is a high level coordination language which allows the definition of a network of cooperating HPF tasks, where each task is assigned to a disjoint set of processors. Tasks interact according to static and predictable patterns and can be composed using predefined structures, called patterns or skeletons, in a declarative way. Besides defining the interaction among tasks, patterns also specify processor and data layouts. DIP is based on the use of domains, i.e. regions together with some interaction information that will allow efficient inter-task coordination.

We have initially established two patterns in DIP. The MULTIBLOCK pattern is focussed on the solution of multi-block and domain decomposition-based problems, which conform an important kind of problems in the high performance computing area. This pattern specifies the different blocks or domains that form the problem and also establishes the coordination scheme among tasks. For the latter role, it defines the borders among domains and establishes the way these borders will be updated.

The other skeleton provided by DIP is the PIPE pattern, which pipelines sequences of tasks in a primitive way. It is also based on the use of domains, which avoids that computational aspects such as data types have to appear at the coordination level, improving pattern reusability. In this case, no border among domains has to be explicitly specified, since all data associated to a domain are involved in the interaction. Nested pipeline patterns are allowed so that complex structures can be built in a declarative way.

HPF tasks receive the domains they need and use them to establish the necessary variables for computation. Local computations are achieved by means of HPF sentences while the communication and synchronization among tasks are carried out through some incorporated DIP primitives (PUT_DATA, GET_DATA, CONVERGE). A new type (DOMAINxD) and a new attribute (GRIDxD) have also been included.

3 Two simple examples

3.1 Example 1. Laplace's equation

The following program shows the MULTIBLOCK pattern for an irregular problem that solves Laplace's equation in two dimensions using Jacobi's finite differences method with 5 points.

$$\Delta u = 0 \quad in \ \Omega \tag{1}$$

where u is a real function, Ω is the domain, a subset of R^2, and Dirichlet boundary conditions have been specified on $\partial\Omega$, the boundary of Ω:

$$u = g \quad in \ \partial\Omega \tag{2}$$

```
MULTIBLOCK Jacobi    u/1,1,Nxu,Nyu/, v/1,1,Nxv,Nyv/
   solve(u:(BLOCK,BLOCK)) ON PROCS(4,4)
   solve(v:(BLOCK,BLOCK)) ON PROCS(2,2)
WITH BORDERS
   u(Nxu,Ny1,Nxu,Ny2) <- v(2,1,2,Nyv)
   v(1,1,1,Nyv) <- u(Nxu-1,Ny1,Nxu-1,Ny2)
END
```

The domains in which the problem is divided are shown in Figure 1 together with a possible data distribution and the border between domains. Dotted lines represent the distribution into each HPF task. A domain definition is achieved

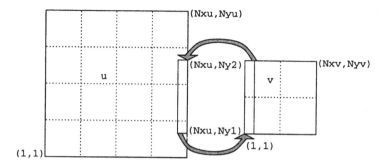

Fig. 1. Communication between two HPF tasks.

by means of an assignment of Cartesian points, i.e. the region of the domain is established. For example, the expression u/1,1,Nxu,Nyu/ assigns to the domain u the region of the plane that extends from the point (1,1) to the point (Nxu,Nyu). A border is specified by means of the <- operator. For example, the expression u(Nxu,Ny1,Nxu,Ny2) <- v(2,1,2,Nyv) indicates that the zone of u delimited by points (Nxu,Ny1) and (Nxu,Ny2) will be updated by the values belonging to the zone of v delimited by points (2,1) and (2,Nyv).

In the task call specification, the name of the domain (say u) to be solved by the task (solve) and the data distribution (for example (BLOCK,BLOCK)) are specified. The processor layout is also indicated (for example ON PROCS(4,4)). The distribution types correspond to those of HPF. This declaration does not perform any data distribution but indicates the future distribution of data associated to the specified domain. The knowledge at the coordination level of data distribution is the key for an efficient implementation of the communication among HPF tasks. A task knows the distribution of its domain and the distribution of every domain with a border in common with its domain by means of the information declared in the pattern. So, it can be deduced which part of the border needs to be sent to which processor of other task. This is achieved at compilation time.

Finally, the code of subroutine solve used for the two tasks specified in the pattern is shown below. Line 2 declares a domain variable for the received domain. Line 3 uses the attribute GRID to declare two record variables g and g_old. After domain and grid declarations, line 4 is a special kind of distribution which produces the distribution of the field DATA (an array of real numbers) and the replication of the field DOMAIN (the associated domain) of both g and g_old variables. In lines 5 and 6, arrays g%DATA and g_old%DATA are dynamically created at the same time that the domain d is assigned to the fields g%DOMAIN and g_old%DOMAIN, respectively. The initialization of g%DATA is performed in the subroutine called in line 7. Statement 9 produces the assignment of the two variables with GRID attribute. Since g_old has its domain already defined, this instruction will just produce a copy of the values of the field g%DATA to g_old%DATA.

Lines 10 and 11 are the first where communication is achieved. Data from g%DATA needed by each task are communicated. Local computation is accomplished by the subroutines called in lines 12 and 13 while the convergence is tested in line 14. The instruction CONVERGE causes a communication between the two tasks. In this case, the communicated data is the value of the variable error. The maximum value (calculated by function maxim) obtained in each process is assigned to the variable error once the execution of CONVERGE is finished.

```
1)subroutine solve (d)
2)DOMAIN2D d
3)double precision,GRID2D :: g,g_old
4)!hpf$ distribute(BLOCK,BLOCK)::g,g_old
5)g%DOMAIN = d
6)g_old%DOMAIN = d
7)call initGrid (g)
8)do i=1, niters
9)   g_old = g
10)   PUT_DATA (g)
11)   GET_DATA (g)
12)   call computeLocal (g, g_old)
13)   error = computeNorm (g, g_old)
14)   CONVERGE (g, error, maxim)
15)   Print *, "Max norm: ", error
16)enddo
17)end subroutine solve
```

3.2   Example 2. 2-D Fast Fourier Transform

2-D FFT transform is probably the application most widely used to demonstrate the usefulness of exploiting a mixture of both task and data parallelism [11][6]. Given an N×N array of complex values, a 2-D FFT entails performing N independent 1-D FFTs on the columns of the input array, followed by N independent 1-D FFTs on its rows. In order to increase the solution performance and scalability, a pipeline solution scheme is preferred as proved in [11] and [6]. Figure 2 shows the array distributions needed for that scheme.

This mixed task and data parallelism scheme can be easily codified using DIP. The following code shows the PIPE pattern. A domain d/1,1,N,N/ is defined for representing the application array at the coordination level. Again, data distribution and processor layout are indicated in the task call specification.

```
PIPE FFT2D
   cfft(d/1,1,N,N/:(*,BLOCK)) ON PROCS(4)
   rfft(d:(BLOCK,*)) ON PROCS(4)
END
```

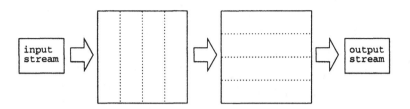

Fig. 2. Array distributions for 2-D FFT.

The code below shows the two stages. The stage **cfft** reads an input element, performs the 1-D transformations and calls PUT_DATA(a). The stage **rfft** calls GET_DATA(b) to receive the array, performs the 1-D transformations and write the result. The communication schedule is known by both tasks, so that a point to point communication between the different HPF processors can be carried out.

```
1)subroutine cfft (d)
2)DOMAIN2D d
3)complex, GRID2D :: a
4)!hpf$ distribute a(*,block)
5)a%DOMAIN= d
6)do i= 1, n_images
7)   call read_stream (a%DATA) ! read input
8)!hpf$ independent
9)   do icol = 1, N
10)    call fftSlice(a%DATA(:,icol))
11)   enddo
12)   PUT_DATA (a)
13)enddo
14)end
```

```
1)subroutine rfft (d)
2)DOMAIN2D d
3)complex, GRID2D :: b
4)!hpf$ distribute b(block,*)
5)b%DOMAIN= d
6)do i= 1, n_images
7)   GET_DATA (b)
8)!hpf$ independent
9)   do irow = 1, N
10)    call fftSlice(b%DATA(irow,:))
11)   enddo
12)   call write_stream (b%DATA) !write output
13)enddo
14)end
```

An alternative solution that shows how nested PIPE patterns are used is given in the following code.

```
PIPE FFT2D INOUT d/1,1,N,N/
  cfft(d:(*,BLOCK)) ON PROCS(4)
  rfft(d:(BLOCK,*)) ON PROCS(4)
END
PIPE Alternative_Solution
  Input(d/1,1,N,N/:(*,BLOCK)) ON PROCS(1)
  FFT2D(d)
  Output(d:(BLOCK,*)) ON PROCS(1)
END
```

A list of input/output domain definitions must appear after the nested pattern name. One of the predefined word IN, OUT, INOUT must precede each domain definition. Here, the domain involved in the pattern FFT2D is defined as an input/output domain. This pattern is "called" in the second stage of the main PIPE pattern. Subroutines cfft and rfft shown above must be modified since read/write operations are now carried out by Input and Output stages. So, line 7 in subroutine cfft is substituted by a call to GET_DATA(a), and line 12 in subroutine rfft is now a call to PUT_DATA(b).

Although the first solution is shorter, the second one establishes a more useful PIPE FFT2D pattern, since it can be reused in more complex applications, such as Convolution, which is a standard technique used to extract feature information from images. It involves two 2-D FFTs, an elementwise multiplication, and an inverse 2-D FFT and it is applied to two streams of input images to generate a single output stream.

4 Implementation Issues and Results

In order to evaluate the performance of DIP, a prototype has been developed. Several examples have been used to test it and the obtained preliminary results have successfully proved the efficiency of the proposal. Here, we show the results for Jacobi's method and the 2-D FFT problem explained above.

For designing our initial prototype, we have built a compiler that translates our DIP code to BCL code. The implementation is based on source-to-source transformations together with the necessary libraries and it has been realized on top of the MPI communication layer and the public domain HPF compilation system ADAPTOR [3]. No change to the HPF compiler has been needed. In a BCL program there are one coordinator process and one or several worker processes. The coordinator process is in charge of establishing all the coordination aspects and creating the worker processes. A worker process is the computational task. So, in our DIP to BCL transformation phase, we have created the coordinator process from the coordination pattern and the worker processes from our computational tasks.

Table 1. HPF/DIP ratio for Jacobi's method

Domains	HPF/DIP ratio		
	4 Procs.	8 Procs.	16 Procs.
2	1.03	1.27	1.49
4	1.04	1.57	2.38
8	0.93	1.57	2.90

Table 2. HPF/DIP ratio for 2-D FFT

Size	HPF/DIP ratio		
	4 Procs.	8 Procs.	16 Procs.
32 by 32	1.59	2.08	1.47
64 by 64	1.09	1.44	1.83
128 by 128	1.03	1.08	1.25

A cluster of 4 nodes DEC AlphaServer 4100 interconnected by means of Memory Channel has been used. Each node has 4 processors Alpha 22164 (300 MHz) sharing a 256 MB RAM memory. The operating system is Digital Unix V4.0D (Rev. 878).

Table 1 reports the ratio between the HPF and DIP execution times for Jacobi's method for the different domains of the problem and numbers of processors exploited. We have considered 2, 4 and 8 domains with a 128×128 grid each one. The program has been executed for 20000 iterations. Table 1 highlights the better performance of the mixed task and data-parallel implementation. When the number of processors is equal to the number of domains (only task parallelism is achieved) DIP has also shown better results. Only when there are more domains than available processors, DIP has shown less performance because of the context change overhead among weight processes.

Table 2 reports the HPF/DIP ratio for different problem sizes of the 2-D FFT application. Again, the performance of DIP is generally better. However, HPF performance is near DIP as the problem size becomes larger and the number of processors decreases, as it also happens in other approaches [11]. In this situation, HPF performance is quite good and so, the integration of task parallelism does not contribute so much.

5 Conclusions

We have used DIP, a Domain Interaction Pattern-based high level coordination language, to integrate task and data parallelism. The suitability and expressiveness of the model have been proved by means of some examples. We have also confirm the efficiency of the approach discussing some experimental results obtained with an initial prototype. The main advantage of this approach is to supply programmers with a concise, pattern-based, high level declarative way to describe the interaction of their HPF tasks. By means of predefined skeletons, the programmer can express task parallelism among a collection of data parallel HPF tasks, so that task and data parallelism integration is achieved. The use of domains and the establishment of data and processor layouts at the coordination level allow pattern reusability and efficient implementations, respectively.

References

1. Agrawal, G., Sussman, A., Saltz, J.: An integrated runtime and compile-time approach for parallelizing structured and block structured applications. IEEE Transactions on Parallel and Distributed Systems, **6(7)** (1995) 747–754
2. Bal, H.E., Haines, M.: Approaches for Integrating Task and Data Parallelism. IEEE Concurrency, **6(3)** (1998) 74–84
3. Brandes, T.: ADAPTOR Programmer's Guide (Version 7.0). Technical documentation, GMD-SCAI, Germany. (1999) `ftp://ftp.gmd.de/GMD/adaptor/docs/pguide.ps`
4. Carriero, N., Gelernter, D.: Coordination Languages and their Significance. Communications of the ACM, **35(2)** (1992) 97–107
5. Chapman, B., Haines, M., Mehrotra, P., Zima, H., Rosendale, J. Opus: A Coordination Language for Multidisciplinary Applications. Scientific Programming, **6(2)** (1997) 345-362
6. Ciarpaglini, S., Folchi, L., Orlando, S., Pelagatti, S., Perego, R.: Integrating Task and Data Parallelism with taskHPF. International Conference on Parallel and Distributed Processing Techniques and Applications (PDPTA'00), Las Vegas, Nevada. (2000) 2485–2492
7. Cole, M., Zavanella, A.: Activity Graphs: A Model-Independent Intermediate Layer for Skeletal Coordination. 15th Annual ACM Symposium on Applied Computing (SAC'00). Special Track on Coordination Models, Villa Olmo, Como, Italy. (2000) 255–261
8. Díaz, M., Rubio, B., Soler, E., Troya, J.M.: BCL: A Border-based Coordination Language. International Conference on Parallel and Distributed Processing Techniques and Applications (PDPTA'00), Las Vegas, Nevada. (2000) 753–760
9. Díaz, M., Rubio, B., Soler, E., Troya, J.M.: DIP: A Pattern-based Approach for Task and Data Parallelism Integration. To appear in 16th Annual ACM Symposium on Applied Computing (SAC'01). Special Track on Coordination Models, Las Vegas, Nevada. (2001)
10. Dinda, P., Gross, T., O'Hallaron, D., Segall, E., Stichnoth, J., Subhlok, J., Webb, J., Yang, B.: The CMU task parallel program suite. Technical Report CMU-CS-94-131, School of Computer Science, Carnegie Mellon University, (1994)
11. Foster, I., Kohr, D., Krishnaiyer, R., Choudhary, A.: A library-based approach to task parallelism in a data-parallel language. J. of Parallel and Distributed Computing, **45(2)** (1997) 148–158
12. High Performance Fortran Forum: High Performance Fortran Language Specification version 2.0 (1997)
13. Koelbel, C., Loveman, D., Schreiber, R., Steele, G., Zosel, M.: The High Performance Fortran Handbook. MIT Press (1994)
14. Orlando S., Perego, R.: $COLT_{HPF}$ A Run-Time Support for the High-Level Coordination of HPF Tasks. Concurrency: Practice and experience, **11(8)** (1999) 407–434

15. Pelagatti, S.: Structured Development of Parallel Programs. Taylor&Francis (1997)
16. Rauber, T., Rünger, G.: A Coordination Language for Mixed Task and Data Parallel Programs. 14th Annual ACM Symposium on Applied Computing (SAC'99). Special Track on Coordination Models, San Antonio, Texas. (1999) 146–155
17. Skillincorn, D.: The Network of Tasks Model. International Conference on Parallel and Distributed Computing and Systems (PDCS'99). Boston, Massachusetts. (1999)
18. Skillincorn, D., Pelagatti, S.: Building Programs in the Network of Tasks Model. 15th Annual ACM Symposium on Applied Computing (SAC'00). Special Track on Coordination Models, Villa Olmo, Como, Italy. (2000) 248–254
19. Subhlok, J., Yang, B.: A New Model for Integrated Nested Task and Data Parallel Programming. 6th ACM SIGPLAN Symposium on Principles and Practice of Parallel Programming (PPoPP'97), Las Vegas, Nevada. (2000) 1–12

Using Loop-Level Parallelism
to Parallelize Vectorizable Programs

D. M. Pressel[1], J. Sahu[2], and K. R. Heavey[2]

[1]U.S. Army Research Laboratory, Computational and Information Sciences Directorate,
Aberdeen Proving Ground, Maryland 21005-5067 USA
dmpresse@arl.mil
[2]U.S. Army Research Laboratory, Weapons and Materials Research Directorate,
Aberdeen Proving Ground, Maryland 21005-5069 USA
{sahu, heavey}@arl.mil

Abstract. One of the major challenges facing high performance computing is the daunting task of producing programs that will achieve acceptable levels of performance when run on parallel architectures. Although many organizations have been actively working in this area for some time, many programs have yet to be parallelized. Furthermore, some programs that were parallelized were done so for obsolete systems. These programs may run poorly, if at all, on the current generation of parallel computers. Therefore, a straightforward approach to parallelizing vectorizable codes is needed without introducing any changes to the algorithm or the convergence properties of the codes. Using the combination of loop-level parallelism, and RISC-based shared memory SMPs has proven to be a successful approach to solving this problem.

Keywords. parallel programming, high performance computer, super computer, loop-level parallelism

1 Introduction

One of the major challenges facing "high performance computing" is the daunting task of producing programs that will achieve acceptable levels of performance when run on parallel architectures.[1] In order to meet this challenge, the program must simultaneously achieve three goals:

1) Achieve a reasonable level of parallel speedup at an acceptable cost.
2) Demonstrate an acceptable level of serial performance so that moderate sized problems do not require enormous levels of resources.
3) Use an algorithm with a high enough level of algorithmic efficiency that the problem remains tractable.

---

[1]This work was made possible through a grant of computer time by the U.S. Department of Defense (DOD) High Performance Computing Modernization Program. The time was spent at the ARL-MSRC, NAVO-MSRC, NRL-DC, TARDEC-DC, and SPAWAR-DC along with smaller amounts of time at other sites. Funding was provided as part of the Common High Performance Computing Software Support Initiative administered by the DOD High Performance Computing Modernization Program.

Even though many organizations have been actively working in this area for 5–10 years (or longer), many programs have yet to be parallelized. Furthermore, some programs that were parallelized, were done so for what are now obsolete systems (e.g., SIMD computers from Thinking Machines and MASPAR), and these programs run poorly, if at all, on the current generation of parallel computers. There has also been a problem that some approaches to parallelization can subtly change the algorithm and result in convergence problems when using large numbers of processors [1]. This is a common problem, particularly when using "domain decomposition" with "implicit" CFD^2 codes. There are algorithmic solutions to this problem (e.g., multigrid codes or the use of a preconditioner); however, many of these solutions have problems in their own right (e.g., poor scalability).

At the other end of the spectrum, there are those who champion automatic parallelization. They expect to soon be able to parallelize production codes for efficient execution on modern production hardware. Unfortunately, as a general rule, this has not happened.

From discussions such as this, talks with numerous researchers, and the authors' research at the U.S. Army Research Laboratory, the following can be concluded:

- Writing parallel programs is a challenge.
- Writing efficient serial programs on today's *RISC* and *CISC* processors with their memory hierarchies (i.e., *cache*) is a challenge.
- Requiring the program to show near-linear scalability out to hundreds/thousands of processors greatly complicates matters.
- Requiring the program to show portable performance across all or most modern parallel architectures greatly complicates matters.
- Modern processors are fast enough that for many problems that have traditionally been considered to be the sole domain of supercomputers, they may now be solvable using a moderate sized system (e.g., 10–100 *GFLOPS* of peak processing power) given a sufficiently efficient algorithm and implementation.

Therefore, a straightforward approach to the parallelization of one or more important classes of codes is needed. This approach will meet the following requirements:

- It will work with a class of machines that has more than one member in it, but it need not include the entire universe of parallel computers.
- It will not require an unreasonable amount of effort.
- The results achieved by using this approach must satisfy the needs of the user community.
- The combined hardware and software costs must be acceptable.
- At least for small- to moderate-sized problems, it must be possible to complete the project before the equipment is obsolete.

The remainder of this paper will begin by discussing an approach developed at the U.S. Army Research Laboratory that was designed to meet all of these requirements for a large and important class of codes. Following this, the results of applying this

---

[2] All items in italics are defined in the Glossary.

approach to a specific production code will be discussed. It will conclude by considering some issues in greater detail and with a discussion of related work.

2 Class of Codes

For this project, the class of codes that was selected was the class of vectorizable codes. Of particular interest were those vectorizable codes that were considered to be nonparallelizable. A representative code was selected (F3D, an implicit CFD code) [2]. The following factors make this class of codes particularly interesting:

- From the mid-1970s to the mid-1990s, the terms vector computers and supercomputers were nearly synonymous (e.g., Cray C90).
- Many of the traditional vectorizable algorithms are known to be computationally more efficient than the algorithms most frequently associated with parallel computing.
- If one can efficiently tune one of these jobs to run on a parallel computer, then any job that exhibits an acceptable level of performance when using one processor of a C90 should exhibit an acceptable level of performance when using a modest number of RISC processors.
- Problem sizes that are ten times greater (that is ten times overall, not ten times in each direction) are likely to exhibit an acceptable level of performance when using a moderate-sized system (e.g., 10–100 GFLOPS of peak processing power).
- In recent years, SGI, SUN, Convex/HP, DEC/Compaq, and IBM have produced *SMPs* with this level of performance.
- It is our belief and experience that many of these systems are extremely well suited for running programs that have been parallelized using "loop-level parallelism" (e.g., OpenMP).
- Since vectorization is a form of loop-level parallelism, there is reason to hope that many vectorizable programs can be parallelized using this technique. While it is not always clear that this will be the best approach to parallelizing these programs, if one focuses on programs that are hard to parallelize, that objection should be effectively eliminated.

Unfortunately, this is not the end of the story. It would be nice if things were this simple, but they are not. Three important obstacles had to be conquered before this project could get off of the ground:

1) Sufficiently powerful SMPs had to come onto the market. At the start of this project, no one had yet produced a RISC-based SMP with a peak speed of 10 GFLOPS, let alone 100 GFLOPS.
2) All RISC processors use caches, and these processors were generally considered to be poorly suited to the needs of running scientific codes [3].
3) Vectorization is normally applied to the inner-most loop of a loop nest. However, as will be seen in section three, when using OpenMP and similar techniques, one is well advised to parallelize outer (or at least middle) loops. In some cases, this will necessitate the interchanging of loops in the loop nest. It

may also be desirable to perform other transformations such as combining loops under a common outer loop.

3 Symmetric Multiprocessors

There are primarily four types of parallel computers in use today:

1) Distributed memory systems. These are also sometimes referred to as "shared nothing." They are almost always programmed using a message-passing library (in recent years, *MPI* has become the standard library).

2) Globally addressable memory. Cray Research frequently referred to the Cray T3D and T3E as shared memory architectures. A more appropriate description is globally addressable memory. While it is true that each processor can access all of the memory associated with a job, there are some important differences between these systems and true shared memory:

   a) The normal load and store instructions that are normally used to access the local memory cannot be used to access the remote memory.

   b) While it is theoretically possible to use the same instructions to perform loads and stores involving both local and remote memory, these instructions are not cache coherent.

   c) The introduction of the synchronization events needed to replace hardware coherency with software coherency can significantly interfere with the performance of the code. Since this requires replacing an automatic function of the hardware with a manual function of the code writer, it can greatly complicate efforts to produce valid code.

3) Master slave. There have been a wide range of these systems produced in the past, including many of the *SIMD*-based systems. For the purpose of this paper, we will only discuss shared memory systems using this organization. Their advantage was that this organization made it easy to port a uniprocessor operating system to a parallel computer. Their disadvantage was that their performance scaled very poorly. As a result, few such systems are still being produced.

4) Symmetric multiprocessor. While more than one type of system might conform to this title, this paper will only use it to refer to shared memory systems in which most, if not all, critical sections of the operating system can run on any of the processors (this is where the term symmetric comes from) [4]. Furthermore, if the processors have one or more levels of cache (as all RISC-based systems do, but which most vector based systems lack), the system is cache coherent (otherwise this paper would refer to it as globally addressable).

Now consider the constraints that the choice of hardware places on the effort to efficiently parallelize a program. When using loop-level parallelism based on the use of compiler directives, there is no need to explicitly generate messages. The data will flow between processors and main memory (in some cases, it will even flow directly between two processors) as needed (for the time being, questions of efficiency in a *NUMA* or *COMA* architecture will be ignored; section 7 will discuss these questions).

Therefore, the main cost of parallelization will be assumed to be the synchronization cost associated with exiting a parallel section of code. On different machines and load factors, the synchronization cost (for scalable systems) ranges from 2,000 to 1 million cycles (or more). From the standpoint of efficiency, one would like to keep these costs below 1% of the runtime. Table 1 shows how many cycles of work must be associated with the loop when run on a single processor in order to achieve this goal. It is important to keep in mind that the synchronization cost is highly dependent on the system load and the design of the memory system but is almost independent of the design of the processor. Therefore, as the memory latency (when expressed in cycles) for a random memory location continues to increase, the synchronization costs would also be expected to increase.

Table 1. The minimum amount of work (in cycles) per parallelized loop required for efficient execution.

Number of processors used	Hypothetical synchronization cost (in cycles)		
	10,000	100,000	1,000,000
2	2,000,000	20,000,000	200,000,000
8	8,000,000	80,000,000	800,000,000
32	32,000,000	320,000,000	3,200,000,000
128	128,000,000	1,280,000,000	12,800,000,000

Two conclusions can be reached from Table 1:
1) It is imperative to minimize the synchronization costs.
2) Every effort should be made to maximize the amount of work per synchronization event (see Table 2).

Table 2 clearly demonstrates the advantage of parallelizing primarily outer loops. It also demonstrates the difficulty associated with the efficient parallelization of boundary condition routines. As such, it is frequently desirable to leave such routines unparallelized. However, for larger numbers of processors, this may result in problems with Amdahl's Law (too much time spent executing serial code).

4 The Approach

Since this approach is predicated on the assumption that one can achieve the desired level of performance when using modest-to-moderate numbers of processors, the first step is to improve the serial efficiency of the code. As was previously stated, the general consensus was that this would be difficult, possibly even impossible, to achieve. However, our experience showed that this need not be the case, which is not

Table 2. The available amount of work (in cycles) per synchronization event for a 1 million grid point zone.

Problem type	Grid dimension	No. of loop iterations	Work per grid point (in cycles)		
			10	100	1000
1-D	1,000,000	1,000,000	10,000,000	100,000,000	1,000,000,000
2-D	1000×1000	1,000			
	Inner loop		10,000	100,000	1,000,000
	Outer loop		10,000,000	100,000,000	1,000,000,000
	Boundary condition		10,000	100,000	1,000,000,000
3-D	100×100×100	100			
	Inner loop		1,000	10,000	100,000
	Middle loop		100,000	1,000,000	100,000,000
	Outer loop		10,000,000	100,000,000	1,000,000,000
	Boundary condition-inner loop		1,000	10,000	100,000
	Boundary condition-outer loop		100,000	1,000,000	100,000,000

to say that the effort could be completed in a few days. There were four main concepts used in this part of the effort:

1) Use a large memory SMP, which was a key enabling factor for this part of the effort. It is easier to perform serial tuning when working with serial code.
2) Use traditional techniques such as reordering of loops and/or array indices, blocking, and matrix transpose operations to increase the locality of reference.
3) Reorder the work so that rather than streaming data into and out of the processor, the code would stress maximizing the amount of work per cache miss.[3]
4) Adjust the size of scratch arrays so that they can be locked into cache. In particular, there were two key loops in F3D that had dependencies in two out of three directions. In order to vectorize these loops, the original programmers had to process data one plane at a time. This meant that the size of the scratch arrays were proportional to the size of a plane of data. Clearly for large problems, these scratch arrays were unlikely to fit into even the largest caches. However, since RISC processors do not rely on vectorization to achieve high levels of performance, it was possible to resize these arrays to hold just a single row or column of a single plane of data. The arrays now comfortably fit in a 1 MB cache for zone dimensions ranging up to about 1000.

---

[3]In this respect, implicit CFD codes have a definite advantage over explicit CFD codes, since they do more work per time step.

Therefore, one can see that while SMPs suffer from a larger memory latency (relative to the memory latency of most workstations and *MPP*s, the presence of large caches can more than make up for this limitation.

Once most of the serial tuning had been completed, it was possible to parallelize the code. Here one of the strengths of loop-level parallelism really shined. With both *HPF* and traditional message passing code, one is generally left with an all or nothing proposition. In other words, either all of the code must be parallelized, or the program will not run at all. When using loop-level parallelism in conjunction with an SMP, this is definitely not the case. Therefore, it is possible to use profiling to find the expensive loops and then to parallelize them one (or a few) at a time. This allows one to alternate between parallelization and debugging, which in most cases will greatly simplify the debugging process. It will also allow one to better judge the effectiveness of what they have tried. In many cases, this will greatly simplify the task of parallelization compared to all-or-nothing approaches such as HPF or using message passing libraries (e.g., MPI). This is not a unique observation, a similar observation was made by Frumkin et al. [5], as well as others.

As previously mentioned, vectorization is a form of loop-level parallelism. Therefore, in theory one should be able to use OpenMP to parallelize vectorizable code. In practice, there are four additional steps that need to be taken if one is to achieve high levels of performance:

1) Since vectorization deals with inner loops, it is generally desirable to parallelize the outer loops, even though they are not involved in the vectorization of the program (see example 1).
2) It is frequently desirable to merge loops together (see example 2). It should be noted that in some cases the merging of loops for purposes of parallelization can be combined with the serial tuning technique of code blocking.
3) In some cases one can significantly improve performance by parallelizing a loop in a parent subroutine (in some cases, one has to first create such a loop) (see example 3). It should be noted that in general this optimization will reduce the number of synchronization events by 1–3 orders of magnitude!
4) One has to be very careful when dealing with arrays that are parts of a common block. When possible, it is desirable to move the arrays out of the common blocks (in some cases, this has to be done during the serial tuning as a first step in the resizing of those arrays).

Two things are important to remember:

1) The more processors that are used, the harder it is to justify the overhead associated with the parallelization of boundary condition subroutines (as well as other inexpensive subroutines).
2) The more time spent in serial code, the harder it is to show benefit from using larger (e.g., 50+) numbers of processors.

Therefore, one is left with the problem of choosing between the lesser of two evils:

1) As the number of processors increases, the speed first peaks and then starts to drop off (assuming that the synchronization costs are a function of the number of processors being used).

```
C$doacross local (L,J,K)
      DO 10 L=1,LMAX
         DO 10 K=1,KMAX
            DO 10 J=1,JMAX
               Some computation with no dependencies in any direction
   10    CONTINUE
```

Example 1. Parallelizing an outer loop.

```
C$doacross local (L,J,K)
      DO 20 L=1,LMAX
         DO 10 K=1,KMAX
            DO 10 J=1,JMAX
               Body of the first loop
   10    CONTINUE
         DO 20 K=1,KMAX
            DO 20 J=1,JMAX
               Body of the second loop
   20    CONTINUE
```

Example 2. Merging loops to reduce synchronization costs.

```
      DO 10 J=1,JMAX
C  NOTE:  We will assume that there are dependencies in the J direction
C  that inhibit parallelization.
         CALL SUBA(...)
C  SUBA batches up a 2-dimensional buffer for processing by SUBB.
         CALL SUBB(...)
C  SUBB has a dependency in one direction, which requires processing a
C  2-dimensional buffer if the code is to be vectorizable.
   10    CONTINUE
```

(a) What the original code looked like.

```
C$doacross local (L,J)
        DO 10 L=1,LMAX
           DO 10 J=1,JMAX
              CALL SUBA(...)
C  SUBA now batches up a 1-dimensional buffer that easily fits in a
C  large cache, for processing by SUBB.
              CALL SUBB(...)
C  SUBB has a dependency in one direction, but since we are no longer
C  dealing with vector processors, this does not matter. Therefore SUBB
C  can safely process the much smaller 1-dimensional buffer.
   10      CONTINUE
```

(b) The cache optimized parallelized code.

Example 3. Parallelizing a parent subroutine.

2) As the number of processors increases, the speed approaches an asymptotic limit.

The net effect of this is that, past a certain point, it is hard to show good speedup when using loop-level parallelism. While the authors are familiar with a number of researchers who felt that this limit would be around 4–16 processors, it is our experience that one should be able to efficiently use 30–128 processors (depending on the problem and the problem size).

Another related problem is that most people are used to thinking in terms of problems that have a nearly infinite level of parallelism. In such cases, the ideal speedup is linear. However, with loop-level parallelism, one is frequently dealing with parallelizing loops that have between 10 and 1000 iterations. This means that the available parallelism is in the range of 10–1000. When the number of processors is within roughly a factor of 10 of the available parallelism, the ideal speedup is no longer linear. Instead the curve shows a distinctly stair-step shape. Table 3 shows where this shape comes from.

Table 3. Predicted speedup for a loop with 15 units of parallelism.

Number of processors	Maximum units of parallelism assigned to a single processor	Predicted speed up
1	15	1.000
2	8	1.875
3	5	3.000
4	4	3.750
5–7	3	5.000
8–14	2	7.500
15	1	15.000

5   Results

We have been able to do serial runs on an SGI Origin 2000 for problem sizes ranging from 1–200 million grid points without a significant decrease in the MFLOPS rate. This is the exact opposite of what was expected based on the literature at the time [3]. Furthermore, serial tuning on the SGI Power Challenge resulted in a speedup of more than a factor of 10. Attempts were made to measure the speedup on a Convex Exemplar SPP-1000. However, even though a 3 million grid point problem was being used, the vector version of the code was running so slowly that the job was killed before it had completed 10 time steps (the way things were going, this would probably have taken the better part of a day or more). The serial-tuned code completed 10 time steps in 70 min.

An interesting outcome from the parallelization of this code is that for larger numbers of processors, the performance as a function of the number of processors used is far from linear. Instead, the curve can best be described as a stair-step. (See section 4 for an explanation of this effect.) When using loop-level parallelism with a 3-dimensional code, there can be dependencies in one or more directions for key loops. With a maximum loop dimension of M, the available parallelism is roughly M. Therefore, one can expect to see jumps in performance at M/5, M/4, M/3, M/2, and M processors. This effect is demonstrated in Table 3 and can be seen in the results in Table 4 (e.g., the nearly flat performance between 48 and 64 processors for the 1 million grid point test case and between 88 and 104 processors for the 59 million grid point test case).

Table 4 shows some representative results for the R12000 based SGI Origin 2000 (128 processors, 300 MHz) and the UltraSPARC II based SUN HPC 10000 (64 processors, 400 MHz).[4] In reporting these results, there is the question of what is the best metric to use. We prefer to avoid speedup, since it fails to describe the actual performance of the code and can actually favor poorly performing codes (the lower the serial performance, the easier it is to show good speedup). From the user's perspective, what really matters are metrics such as run time and turn around time. However, as the number of processors approach the available parallelism, the predicted run time should asymptotically approach some low value, making it difficult to evaluate the performance of the code. Our preferred metric is "time steps/hour," since it allows the user to easily estimate what the run time should be (not counting start up and termination costs, which have been eliminated from our results). This metric also has the advantage that for problems with large amounts of parallelism, it gives the linear performance curve that one normally equates with parallel programs. Another useful metric which has been included in Table 4 is the delivered MFLOPS, which allows one to determine not only the parallel efficiency, but also the serial efficiency of our implementation. The peak speed of a processor on the SUN system is 800 MFLOPS and 600 MFLOPS on the SGI system. From the results, one can see that the per processor delivered performance of the two systems is actually very similar. This is probably the result of the two vendors taking different approaches in designing their chips. Some vendors prefer to make the fastest chips possible, even though they have a lot of hazards that can limit their delivered performance, while other vendors prefer to make somewhat slower but friendlier chips. Both approaches are valid and can result in a good product. But as our results demonstrate, it is important to compare products based on their delivered performance, not their peak performance.

---

[4]On the SGI Origin the C$doacross directives were used. On the SUN HPC 10000, the SUN specific PCF directives were used, since at the time SUN did not support either SGI's C$doacross directives or the OpenMP directives.

Table 4. Measured performance of the RISC-optimized shared memory version of F3D.

Number of processors used	Problem size (million grid points)	Performance			
		SUN HPC 10000		SGI R12000 Origin 2000	
		Time steps/hr	MFLOPS	Time steps/hr	MFLOPS
1	1[a]	138	1.80E2	181	2.37E2
32	1	2786	3.64E3	2877	3.76E3
48	1	3093	4.04E3	3545	3.63E3
64	1	2819	3.69E3	3694	4.83E3
72	1	N/A	N/A	4105	5.37E3
88	1	N/A	N/A	5087	6.65E3
1	59[b]	2.3	1.79E2	2.3	1.79E3
32	59	51	3.97E3	59	4.59E3
48	59	74	5.76E3	73	5.68E3
64	59	83	6.56E3	91	7.08E3
72	59	N/A	N/A	101	7.86E3
88	59	N/A	N/A	128	9.96E3
104	59	N/A	N/A	131	1.02E4
112	59	N/A	N/A	144	1.12E4
120	59	N/A	N/A	150	1.17E4
124	59	N/A	N/A	153	1.19E4

[a]The 1 million grid point test case consists of three zones with dimensions of 15×75×70, 87×75×70, and 89×75×70.

[b]The 59 million grid point test case consists of three zones with dimensions of 29×450×350, 173×450×350, and 175×450×350.

6 Tools

In performing the serial tuning, the principle tools used were various profiling tools. Initially, this meant using prof with and without pixie. Without pixie, prof would measure the actual run time for the individual subroutines. With pixie, prof would measure the theoretical run time for the subroutines, assuming an infinitely fast memory system. By subtracting those two sets of numbers, one can then estimate the cost of cache and *TLB* misses. Fortunately, most of today's systems come with tools that allow one to directly measure those values (on systems lacking those tools, codes can be instrumented using PAPI, which is being developed at the University of Tennessee, Knoxville, TN, as a project for the PTOOLS organization).

After tuning for cache and TLB misses, a few loops had a low cache/TLB miss rate but were still expensive to run. Additional hand optimizations guided by assembly code dumps were performed to achieve a higher data reuse rate at the register level while eliminating unnecessary register spilling, pipeline stalls, and low instruction issue rates from excessive numbers of loads and stores. A key aspect of this phase of the tuning was to run the program on as wide a range of RISC-based systems as possible to better understand which optimizations would be of universal value. Table 5 contains a list of systems used in this effort. Using this wide range of systems and compilers allowed tuning for a wider range of TLB and cache sizes. It also allowed us to better anticipate what types of codes current production compilers could handle without producing performance problems.

Table 5. Systems used in tuning/parallelizing the RISC-optimized shared memory version of F3D.

SGI R4400 based Challenge and Indigo 2
SGI R8000 and R10000 based Power Challenges
SGI R10000 and R12000 based Origin 2000s
SUN SuperSPARC based SPARCCenter 2000
SUN Ultra SPARC II based HPC 10000
Convex HP PA-7100 based SPP-1000 and HP PA-7200 based SPP-1600
HP PA-8500 based V-Class

Another key aspect of this effort was to validate the results [7]. There were several stages to this effort, ranging from quick and dirty tests involving only a few time steps, to more elaborate tests performed on fully converged solutions, to finally a complete manual review of the code as part of a formal validation and verification exercise. Unfortunately, when performing some of the intermediate level tests, a mistake that had been introduced into the code would sometimes be found. One of the most useful tools for locating these mistakes was to update the version number of the code daily so that one could go back and find which was the first version to have the bug. One could then use "diff" to identify what the differences were between that version of the code and the previous one. In most cases, this was sufficient in rapidly identifying and fixing the bug (in all of the affected versions). One extreme example of applying this technique occurred early on. In reordering the indices of several key arrays throughout the program, changing almost every executable line of code in the entire program became necessary. Furthermore, all of the lines had to be changed at the same time. Unfortunately, the odds of getting this right proved to be vanishingly small. Additionally, manual inspection of the code failed to find the problems. Fortunately, after going through the entire exercise a second time, we were able to diff the two modified versions of the code, locate the mistakes, and get a code that produced the correct answers in about half the time as the previous version of the code.

The principle tools used for evaluating the performance of the parallelized code were various versions of profiling tools (e.g., Speed Shop on the SGI sytems, CXPERF on the Convex and HP systems, and Loop Tool on the SUN HPC 10000). The tools, in combination with simply timing the runs for various combinations of problem sizes, numbers of processors, and systems, allowed us to identify the issues that affected parallel speedup. The single biggest issue was that since parallelization was being done incrementally, we needed to know which loops were expensive enough to justify being parallelized (both in terms of the effort and additional overhead that would be introduced). Once this was well in hand, the main remaining issue was to understand how the variable costs associated with memory latency and bandwidth in a NUMA environment were affecting the code performance. Unfortunately, experience indicated that not all NUMA platforms were created equal, and these performance problems on the Convex Exemplars were never satisfactorily solved. Fortunately, the results on the SGI system and the SUN HPC 10000 were much better, in part due to all of the work done to try to make the code perform better on the Convex Exemplar [6].

7 The Effect of the NUMA Architecture

With memory latencies ranging from 310–945 NS in a 128 processor SGI Origin 2000 [8], without using any form of out-of-order execution and/or prefetching, one will see a range of usable preprocessor bandwidths of 412 MB/second down to 135 MB/second. Clearly for a shared memory program with a poor cache hit rate and a high proportion of off node accesses, this will result in a significant performance problem. One potential solution is to make use of out-of-order execution and/or prefetching to overlap cache misses in an attempt to achieve a lower effective memory latency. Unfortunately, the maximum per processor usable bandwidth for off node accesses is estimated to be only 195 MB/second, which severely limits the effectiveness of this approach. Our solution to this problem was to produce a highly tuned code with a low enough cache miss rate that the NUMA nature of the Origin 2000 did not matter. According to the output of Perfex when our code is run on a 180 MHz R10000 based Origin 2000 using a single processor, we have only 68 MB/second of memory traffic. Since this is far less than the 135–195 MB/second of usable bandwidth for off node accesses on the Origin 2000, we have been able to treat the Origin 2000 as though it had Uniform Memory Access. Unfortunately, this approach did not work nearly as well on the more heavily NUMA systems such as the Convex Exemplar.

This is not to say that the memory systems on the SGI Origin 2000 and the SUN HPC 10000 did not cause problems. The traditional shared memory systems (e.g., the Cray C90 or the SGI Power Challenge) store data in small blocks or lines, with successive blocks or lines being interleaved between multiple memory banks. On some systems, the size of a block may be as small as a single word (e.g., 8 bytes), while on most cache based systems, a cache line would be treated as a single block (e.g., 64 or 128 bytes). On systems which group memory and processors into nodes (e.g., the SGI Origin 2000, the SUN HPC 10000, and the hypernodes on the Convex Exemplar), the unit of interleaving becomes a page of memory (e.g., 4–16 KB). In that case, one can easily have data from the same page being shared by multiple processors. In extreme cases, this will result in a severe amount of contention with a resulting drop in performance. It is important to note that no amount of page migration will solve this problem—neither will data placement directives. Data replication/caching can help. But the best solution is to initially avoid the problem. It is also interesting to note that as far as the authors know, there are no tools that will identify this problem. The best way to identify the problem now is to profile fixed size runs with varying numbers of processors and look for subroutines that are consuming additional CPU cycles as the number of processors increases. Using tools such as Perfex or Speedshop can determine if the number of cache misses is remaining relatively constant. If this is the case, then one almost certainly has a problem with contention. Example 4 illustrates the three cases (ideal, acceptable, and unacceptable) of concern. Please note that even though Example 4c is using a STRIDE-N access pattern to batch up the buffer, it can still have an acceptable cache miss rate. Unfortunately, the process of batching up the buffer can result in an unacceptable amount of contention on some of these systems. To confuse matters further, and for reasons that the authors were never able to fully explain, the SGI Origin 2000 and the SUN HPC 10000 exhibited this problem under different conditions, thereby making it necessary to eliminate all instances of this type of code from the program.

```
        DIMENSION A(JMAX,KMAX,LMAX)
C$doacross local (J,K,L)
        DO 10 L=1,LMAX
           DO 10 K=1,KMAX
              DO 10 J=1,JMAX
                 A(J,K,L) = ...
   10   CONTINUE
```

(a) An example of the best possible access ordering.

```
        DIMENSION A(JMAX,KMAX,LMAX)
C$do across local (K,J,L)
        DO 10 K=1,KMAX
           DO 10 L=1,LMAX
              DO 10 J=1,JMAX
                 A(J,K,L) = ...
   10 CONTINUE
```

(b) An example of an acceptable, but less desirable ordering.

```
        DIMENSION A(JMAX,KMAX,LMAX), BUFFER(KMAX)
C$doacross local (J,L,K,BUFFER)
        DO 20 J=1,JMAX
           DO 20 L=1,LMAX
              DO 10 K=1,KMAX
                 BUFFER = A(J,K,L)
   10         CONTINUE
              DO 20 K=1,KMAX
                 Perform extensive calculations using BUFFER
   20   CONTINUE
```

(c) An example of an unacceptable ordering.

Example 4. The effect of memory access patterns on contention.

8 Related Work

The simplest approach to using loop-level parallelism is to use an automatic parallelizing compiler. Unfortunately, as Michael Wolfe (the author of "High Performance Compilers for Parallel Computing," Addison-Wesley, 1996) has pointed out—"parallelizing compilers don't work and they never will [9]." A slightly more sophisticated approach has been suggested by Dixie Hisley of the U.S. Army Research Laboratory. This approach uses a combination of compiler directives and hand tuning to parallelize those expensive loops which the automatic parallelizing compilers are unable to handle on their own. The remaining loops are left for the compiler to figure out. In some cases, this was shown to increase the scalability of the code from 8 to 16 processors, with little or no additional work over the use of compiler directives (e.g., C$doacross) and hand tuning on their own. In contrast, using only an automatic parallelizing compiler in this case actually produced parallel slowdown [10].

An excellent comparison using the combination of hand tuning, automatic parallelization, and compiler directives, to the HPF and CAPTools parallelization tools was presented at SC98 [5]. It found that all three approaches had merit, although none would produce good results when used on a fully automatic basis. In many cases, the results from using compiler directives (e.g., C$doacross or CAPTools specific directives) were as good as those produced by hand parallelizing the code using MPI.

Marek Behr attempted to parallelize the F3D program on the Cray T3D using the CRAFT programming model. Unfortunately, this effort had to be abandoned due to poor levels of performance (something that was a common complaint with this programming model) [11]. He then proceeded to manually parallelize the code using message passing calls (SHMEM on the Cray T3D, Cray T3E, and SGI Origin 2000, and MPI on other platforms) to implement loop-level parallelism. While this approach worked and produced a credible level of performance, it was significantly more difficult to implement. Furthermore, because many of the target platforms (e.g., the Cray T3D, Cray T3E, and IBM SP with the Power 2 Super Chip) had caches ranging in size from 16–128 KB, it was impossible to perform many of the cache optimizations that we performed using caches with 1–8 MB of memory [12].

An approach similar to the one we used in tuning and parallelizing F3D was used by James Taft a NASA Ames Research Center to tune and parallelize the ARC3D code for the SGI Origin 2000 [13]. More recently, Mr. Taft has used multiple levels of shared memory parallelism (MLP)—an approach that he has successfully demonstrated with the Overflow code and more recently, several other commonly used codes at NASA Ames Research Center [14,15]. Straight loop-level parallelism and MLP appear to be complementary techniques, each with their own strengths and weaknesses.

There is also a significant body of research involving the use of software distributed shared memory [16]. Unfortunately, there is generally a significant performance penalty when using these systems, which keeps them from being widely accepted for production environments. One of the key problems is that modern SMP and MPP systems usually have per processor memory bandwidths ranging from

200 MB/second to over 1 GB/second, with memory latencies of 100–1000 NS. In contrast, the communications bandwidth for most workstation clusters and many MPPs is rarely much better than 100 MB/second on a per processor basis, with a latency that is frequently in the range of 50–100 microseconds for the better systems (Note that the primary exception to this rule is the Cray T3E when using SHMEM). Attempting to maintain coherency with the 128 byte granularity used in the SGI Origin 2000 with a latency of 100 microseconds results in a per processor bandwidth for off node accesses of 1.3 MB/second. For programs that are parallelized in more than one direction and therefore inevitably have a high level of off node memory accesses, this low level of performance is virtually impossible to overcome on today's high performance systems. Even in hardware implementations of a COMA environment, keeping all of the processors for a single job on a single node is highly desirable [17].

9 Conclusion

It was demonstrated that careful tuning at the implementation level can make a significant difference in the performance of code running on RISC-based systems. Furthermore, it was shown that there are two key enabling technologies for this effort:

1) Large caches.

2) Access to a large amount of main memory, something that SMPs excel at.

Additionally, it was shown that the use of loop-level parallelism can be of significant benefit when trying to parallelize certain classes of vectorizable code. However, several limitations to this approach were discussed:

- The need for sufficiently large and powerful SMPs.
- The importance of tuning the code for a high level of serial efficiency.
- The limitations on scalability (overhead, Amdahl's Law, stair stepping).

In summary, the combination of loop-level parallelism and SMPs represents a powerful tool for the parallelization of vectorizable programs. As long as everyone understands the inherent limitations, it should have a most productive future.

Glossary

CFD	Computational Fluid Dynamics
Cache	a small high speed memory that sits between the processor and main memory, which is designed to store values that are likely to be needed by the processor in the very near future.
CISC	Complicated Instruction Set Computer
COMA	Cache Only Memory Architecture
GFLOPS	Giga Floating-Point Operations Per Second
HPF	High Performance Fortran
NUMA	Non Uniform Memory Access

MPI	Message Passing Interface
MPP	Massively Parallel Processor
RISC	Reduced Instruction Set Computer
SIMD	Single Instruction Multiple Data
SMP	Symmetric Multiprocessor
TLB	Translation Lookaside Buffer

References

[1] Wang, G., and Tafti, D. K.: Performance Enhancement on Microprocessors With Hierarchical Memory Systems for Solving Large Sparse Linear System. International Journal of Supercomputing Applications (1997)

[2] Steger, J. L., Ying, S. X., and Schiff, L. B.: A Partially Flux-Split Algorithm for Numerical Simulation of Compressible Inviscid and Viscous Flows. Proceedings of the Workshop on CFD. Davis, California (1986)

[3] Bailey, D. H.: Microprocessors and Scientific Computing. Proceedings of Supercomputing 93. Los Alamitos, California (1993)

[4] Schimmel, C.: UNIX Systems for Modern Architectures, Symmetric Multiprocessing, and Caching for Kernel Programmers. Addison-Wesley Publishing Company, Reading, Massachusetts (1994)

[5] Frumkin, M., Hribar, M., Jin, H., Waheed, A., and Yan, J.: A Comparison of Automatic Parallelization Tools/Compilers on the SGI Origin 2000. Proceedings for the SC98 Conference. Supercomp Organization, IEEE Computer Society, and ACM (1998)
http://www.supercomp.org/sc98/TechPapers

[6] Pressel, D. M.: Results From the Porting of the Computational Fluid Dynamics Code F3D to the Convex Exemplar (SPP-1000 and SPP-1600), ARL-TR-1923. U.S. Army Research Laboratory, Aberdeen Proving Ground, Maryland (1999)

[7] Edge, H. L., Sahu, J., Sturek, W. B., Pressel, D. M., Heavey, K. R., Weinacht, P., Zoltani, C. K., Nietubicz, C. J., Clarke, J., Behr, M., Collins, P.: Common High Performance Computing Software Support Initiative (CHSSI) Computational Fluid Dynamics (CFD) Project Final Report: ARL Block-Structured Gridding Zonal Navier-Stokes Flow (ZNSFLOW) Solver Software, ARL-TR-2084. U.S. Army Research Laboratory, Aberdeen Proving Ground, Maryland (2000)

[8] Laudon, J., and Lenoski, D.: The SGI Origin: A ccNUMA Highly Scalable Server. Proceedings of the 24th Annual International Symposium on Computer Architecture (ISCA '97), Denver, Colorado. June 2–4, 1997. IEEE Computer Society, Los Alamitos, California

[9] Theys, M. D., Braun, T. D., and Siegel, H. J.: Widespread Acceptance of General-Purpose, Large-Scale Parallel Machines: Fact, Future, or Fantasy? IEEE Concurrency Parallel, Distributed, and Mobile Computing, Vol. 6, No.1 (1998)

[10] Hisley, D. M., Agrawal, G., and Pollock, L.: Performance Studies of the Parallelization of a CFD Solver on the Origin 2000. Proceedings for the 21st Army Science Conference. Department of the Army (1998)

[11] Oberlin, S.: Keynote Address at the International Symposium on Computer Architecture (ISCA '99) (1999) At the time, S. Oberlin had been the Vice President for Software at SGI, having previously been the Vice President for Hardware.

[12] Behr, M., Pressel, D. M., and Sturek, W. B., Jr.: Comments on CFD Code Performance on Scalable Architectures. Computer Methods in Applied Mechanics and Engineering, Vol. 190 (2000) 263–277

[13] Taft, J.: Initial SGI Origin 2000 Tests Show Promise for CFD Codes. NAS News, Vol. 2, No. 25. NASA Ames Research Center (1997)

[14] Taft, J. R.: Shared Memory Multi-Level Parallelism for CFD, Overflow-MLP: A Case Study. Presented at the Cray User Group Origin 2000 Workshop, Denver, Colorado, October 11–13, 1998

[15] Taft, J. R.: Achieving 60 GFLOP/S on the Production CFD CODE OVERFLOW-MLP. Presented at WOMPAT 2000, Workshop on OpenMP Applications and Tools, San Diego, California, July 6–7, 2000

[16] Keleher, P., Cox, A. L., Dwarkadas, S., and Zwaenepoel, W.: TreadMarks: Distributed Shared Memory on Standard Workstations and Operating Systems. Proceedings of the Winter 94 Usenix Conference (1994)
http://www.cs.rice.edu/~willy/TreadMarks/papers.html

[17] Hagersten, E., and Koster, M.: WildFire: A Scalable Path for SMPs. Proceedings of the 5th International Symposium on High-Performance Computer Architecture (HPCA), Orlando, Florida, January 9–13, 1999. IEEE Computer Society, Los Alamitos, California

A Generic C++ Framework for Parallel Mesh-Based Scientific Applications

Jens Gerlach, Peter Gottschling, and Uwe Der

RWCP Parallel and Distributed Systems GMD Laboratory
GMD FIRST, Kekuléstr. 7, 12489 Berlin, Germany, www.first.gmd.de/promise,
{jens,pg,uweder}@first.gmd.de

Abstract. The objects that occur in scientific applications can be classified into *spatial structures*, e.g. meshes, grids, or graphs, and *(numerical) data* that are *associated* with these structures, e.g. grid functions and (sparse) matrices. Our C++ template library Janus rests on the observation that the spatial structures are conceptually *more stable* than the associated data. Janus provides a conceptual framework and generic components for mesh-based scientific applications. An outstanding feature of Janus is its unified treatment of regular and irregular structures. Our library has been developed using the paradigm of *generic programming* and is portably implemented on top of the Standard Template Library. It runs on top of MPI, but it can also be put onto other parallel platforms.

1 Introduction

Many scientific computing applications, like finite element simulations, are based on spatial structures with which various data are associated. These spatial structures may be sets of points, edges or triangles, for instance, and are referred to as *domains* in this work. The associated data are simulation values, like the temperature at each point or the pressure in each cell.

The coherence of domains is specified by relations. There are different kinds of relations: for instance nearest neighbor relations and hierarchical relations as they occur in multilevel methods. Relations and (sparse) matrices that are associated to them describe the communication that occur in scientific applications.

The spatial structures of scientific applications are often irregular. Developing an architecture-neutral, application-oriented framework of reusable software components for them, is an important and very challenging task. PETSc [1], for example, is such a framework that runs on top of MPI. However, since it is written in the C programming language, application data types cannot be directly plugged into it. Providing a well-designed C++ template library would allow this. More application-oriented approaches, such as POOMA [7] or SAMRAI [3], limit themselves to (nested) grids or *structured* adaptive mesh refinement.

Other C++ template libraries whose design follows the paradigm of generic programming can combine expressiveness, reusability, and, last but not least, efficiency, which is of paramount importance for many scientific applications. Convincing examples are the Matrix Template Library (MTL) [12] and the Generic Graph Component Library (GGCL) [9].

Our C++ template library Janus applies this very promising approach to the task of developing *reusable components for the efficient representation of potentially distributed data structures* of mesh-based scientific applications. Janus rests on the observation that the spatial structures are *prior* to the associated data and also *more stable* than these.

An important part of applying the paradigm of generic programming to a particular application domain is *concept development*. In section 2, we give an overview of the three fundamental concepts of Janus—Domain, Relation, and Domain Function. The main template classes of Janus are presented in section 3. There, we also explain how the concepts of Two Phase Domain and Two Phase Relation allow the efficient implementation of data structures for irregular problems. In section 4, we sketch how Janus components can be used for the parallel implementation of a two-dimensional adaptive finite element simulation. Our implementation also includes the repartitioning of the locally refined mesh to ensure that the computational load is balanced.

2 Conceptual Framework

Janus is a C++ template library that simplifies the fast and efficient implementation of finite element and other mesh or grid-based methods. Janus provides not only reusable components but also an extensible conceptual framework to deal efficiently with complex structures of scientific computations.

The design of Janus is based on the paradigm of *generic programming* [10] that became well-known through the C++ Standard Template Library (STL) [14].

2.1 Main Concepts of Janus

In contrast to the STL, we do not deal with fundamental data structures and algorithms of computer science. Rather, we devise concepts that are useful for the representation of sets, their relations, and the data defined on them. In particular, our concepts shall fit the requirements of parallel adaptive mesh methods, that is, they must allow *fast* and *flexible* implementations.

The three fundamental concepts of Janus are Domain, Relation, and Domain Function.

The concepts Domain and Relation contain general requirements that are necessary to describe spatial structures. Basically, a domain is a finite set represented as a sequence. Every element of a domain has a unique *position* (its sequence index) by which it can be represented. This has several important consequences.

It allows to represent data that are associated with a domain by a random access container of the same size as the underlying domain. This property is utilized in the concept Domain Function of Janus.

Relations between domains can be represented by adjacency matrices. A key point of the Janus Relation concept is that it maintains both the application-oriented view of a relation and its efficient linear-algebraic representation. We require that Relation provides several methods (e.g. pull, push) for communicating data associated with the domains of a relation. The semantics of these methods is based on matrix vector multiplications.

2.2 One Phase and Two Phase Structures

To deal with different dynamic requirements to domains, we distinguish between *One Phase Domains* and *Two Phase Domains*. This differentiation applies also to the concept Relation.

Objects that represent complex. i.e., irregular spatial structures usually cannot be completely described at initialization time. They need an *insertion phase* (as a kind of *extended* initialization). In order to enable an *efficient* implementation, we require that these elements contained in such objects may only be retrieved after the insertion phase has been completed. Thus, we have a second phase (called retrieval phase) for these objects and we generally refer to them as *two-phase structures*. Two-phase structures have a method freeze whose call marks the transition from the insertion phase to the retrieval phase.

We use the idea of one and two-phase structures to define *refinements* of our Domain and Relation concepts. Their requirements and practically interesting models are outlined in the following section.

Simple (regular) spatial structures, like rectangular grids, can be completely described at initialization time. There is no need of an insertion phase for them and their elements can be immediately retrieved. Since they have only a retrieval phase but no insertion phase, we refer to them as *one-phase structures*.

3 The C++ Template Library Janus

The template classes of Janus are models of the concepts that have been outlined in section 2. The components of Janus can be used to efficiently implement a variety of applications ranging from simple finite difference methods on rectangular grids to adaptive mesh refinement codes. Figure 1 gives an overview of the template classes currently offered by Janus.

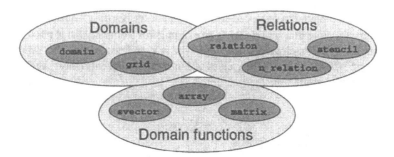

Fig. 1. Components of Janus

Since Janus concepts have only been informally introduced, we combine the introduction of the main template classes with a short specification of the most important concept requirements. More details can be found in the technical report [6].

Most of the components of Janus can be used both within strictly sequential *and* parallel programming contexts. For the latter, it is assumed that Janus is part of an MPI [13] program. A user of Janus must specify at compile time in which mode the library shall be used. For this, there are the C-preprocessor flags _JANUS_SEQ_ and _JANUS_MPI_.

3.1 Domain Classes

The concept Domain describes a set of n different objects that are numbered from 0 to $n - 1$. So in fact, a domain D is a *finite sequence*

$$(d_0, d_1, \ldots, d_{n-1}) \tag{1}$$

with the additional requirement that the mapping $i \mapsto d_i$ is one-to-one.

A type X that is a model of the concept Domain must provide the nested types value_type and size_type and the methods size, operator[] (returns the ith element) and position (the inverse method to operator[]). The operator[] must be a constant time operation. The method position shall not be more complex than $O(\log(n))$ where n is the number of elements of the domain.

Janus currently offers two template classes that are models of the concept Domain. They are the grid<N> and domain<T> (see subsection 3.1) template classes.

The template class domain can be used for irregular domains whose elements are explicitly enumerated. This template is a two-phase domain, which means that there is an explicit *insertion* phase.

When an element is inserted into a domain, mapping information can be specified (using method insert_at). The elements are distributed according to this mapping only when the freeze method is called. Therefore, only few large messages have to be sent instead of many small ones. This shows how two-phase structures enable the efficient implementation of distributed data structures.

The grid template is a one-phase domain and describes the Cartesian product of N integer intervals. Note that grid<N> is an example for a domain that is not a container, i.e., it does not store its elements. Its value type is svector<int,N>. The template svector<T,N> is a special utility class of Janus that represents (short) vectors whose size is known at compile time (see section 3.3).

3.2 Relation Classes

The concept of a *Relation R between two domains* is based on the mathematical concept of a relation between the two sets: A relation is a subset of the cross product of two sets. Since we have a one-to-one correspondence between the domain elements and their positions, we can represent a relation by its *adjacency matrix* M_R.

We give a very short description of currently three relation classes available: stencil for regular relations on grids and the more general types n_relation and relation (see section 3.2).

Relations and Communication The communication patterns of scientific applications are closely related to the adjacency matrix M_R. We only mention the sparsity pattern of the system matrix of a finite element method or the interpolation and restriction operations within mesh hierarchies. In Janus, this knowledge is formalized and put into the requirements of the Relation concept.

Beside the fact that Relation is a refinement of the concept domain (its value type is "pair of integers"), we require that a model of the concept relation provides several matrix-vector operations. The most important of them are `pull` (multiplication with M_R) and `push` (multiplication with the transpose of M_R).

First of all, we note that `pull` and `push` are *member templates* (a relatively new feature of C++) of the relation classes. The parameters of the two template member methods must provide random access to elements of domain functions. Typically, they will hold objects of type `int`, `double`, or `complex<float>`.

Janus also requires the more general `pull_matrix`, `push_matrix`, `gather` and `scatter` template members by a model of the concept Relation. The difference between `pull` and `pull_matrix` is that `pull` multiplies with the adjacency matrix (which has only entries such as 0 or 1) whereas `pull_matrix` uses a matrix with arbitrary coefficients on the *pattern* of the relation. The same holds for the transpose matrix operations `push` and `push_matrix`, respectively. The `gather` method *lifts* data that are associated with a domain onto a relation. In contrast, the `scatter` method projects data associated to a relation onto second domain factor of the relation.

The template class `n_relation<dom1,dom2,Gen>` represents a relation between two domains that can be described by the function object Gen. By *regular*, we mean a relation between two domains where each element of the first domain is in relation with a fixed number n of elements of the second domain. The adjacency matrix of such a relation is more compact than in the case of `relation`. A typical example is the triangle-edge relation of a triangulation: each triangle has exactly three edges.

The template class `relation<dom1,dom2>` describes a potentially irregular relation between two domains. The `relation` template is a model of the concept Two-Phase Relation. This means that it provides an extended initialization phase that is finished only when the `freeze` method is called. Internally, the relation is represented using in the compressed row storage (CRS) format which allows an efficient sparse matrix vector multiplication, i.e. the `pull` and `push` methods.

3.3 Domain Function Classes

Spatial structures are represented by domains and relations between them. The core of scientific computations, however, is usually performed with data that are associated with these spatial structures. The reader shall think for example of pressure and velocity values that are related to grid components and to (sparse) matrices associated with relations.

The concept Domain Function describes objects of a type T that are associated to the elements of a domain d. If d consists of n elements then a domain function d provides random access to n objects of T.

This definition exploits the fact that there is a one-to-one relation between the elements of a domain and their positions. It also allows to use various types of data structures to represent a domain function, e.g., it is possible to use a C-array or the standard container type `std::vector<T>` to represent a domain function of values of type T.

Janus provides the template class `array<Dom,T>` for domain functions related to proper domains and the (sparse) matrix template `matrix<Rel,T>`.

4 A Sample Finite Element Problem

In this section, we show in some detail how a two-dimensional finite element method can be implemented using components of the Janus framework. The complete description can be found in [5].

For sake of simplicity, we consider the homogeneous Poisson problem. We deploy linear triangle finite elements which means that the domain of the boundary value problem is subject to a triangulation and that the corresponding finite element space is spanned by functions that are continuous and element-wise linear polynomials.

We use a cascadic conjugate gradient method [4] to solve the discretized problem. This method works with a hierarchy of meshes. We obtain this hierarchy by successive adaptive refinement that rests on a simple gradient error indicator. The coarse algorithmic structure of our solution method can be seen in figure 2.

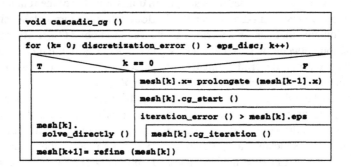

Fig. 2. Nassy Shneiderman diagram of the cascadic CG method

As the reader can see in figure 2, there are several numerical operations performed between two mesh refinement steps. This is a good example for the relative stability of the spatial structures compared to the data defined on them.

In the following subsections we have a closer look at the various computational steps performed in our finite element method.

4.1 Construction of the Finite Element Space

The construction of the finite element space requires at first a triangulation of the given domain. An example is given in figure 3.

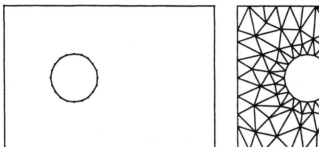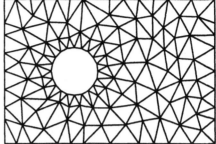

Fig. 3. Test domain that was triangulated using *Triangle* [11]

Vertex and Triangle Sets For the case at hand, the mesh is given by the set of triangles T and the set of vertices V. The node set N, i.e. the set that indexes the basis functions of the finite element space coincides for linear triangle elements with the set of vertices V. The two sets T and V are needed to define the functions that occur during the computations.

One way to represent mesh components is to use natural numbers to name the vertices and to represent a triangle as the triple of its vertices. This representation is also used by the mesh generator *Triangle* [11]. To represent triangles, we use the svector template class of Janus (see section 3.3). Since both the vertices and triangles have to be explicitly stored, we use the domain template (see section 3.1) to define types that represent the sets of vertices and triangles of our mesh.

Important Mesh Relations Various relations between the discrete sets T and V must be maintained since they are used to express the computations that involve functions on the different sets. For the problem at hand, we need the following two relations: the triangle-vertex relation R_{TV} which assigns to each triangle its three vertices and the nearest-neighbor relation R_{VV}. For the representation of the triangle-vertex relation, we can deploy the template class n_relation (see section 3.2). This relation can be set up in the constructor by a user-specified generator. Here the generator triangle_vertex_gen implements the association of the three vertices of a triangle with this triangle.

The nearest-neighbor relation R_{VV} is fundamental for the description of the discrete operator A_n, i.e. this relation defines the matrix sparsity of the linear system. This relation is defined as the set of all pairs of nodes for which an element (i.e. triangle) exists that contains both nodes

$$R_{VV} = \bigcup_{t \in T} \bigcup_{i,j=0}^{2} \{(v_i, v_j) \mid (t, v_0, v_1, v_2) \in R_{TV}\}. \tag{2}$$

This relation is stored as Janus' most general relation class relation and set up by inserting explicitly each pair of vertices that belongs to the same triangle.

4.2 Solution of the Linear System

To solve the linear equations, we use the diagonally scaled CG method. As a side effect of the adaptive mesh refinement, we get a hierarchy of linear equations, which can be utilized in multilevel solvers. For example, we can expand the CG method to a cascadic CG method by using the solution of the linear equation on a certain mesh as an initial guess on the next finer mesh (resp. the interpolated vector). This starting vector lies close to the solution, and the remaining error components are of high frequency (cf. [4]), i.e., they can be reduced with high convergence and the number of CG iterations on the individual levels is limited.

In the following, we present first performance results. Table 1 shows the mesh sizes over three levels of refinement.

Table 1. Progression of mesh sizes through three levels of refinement

Mesh	Vertices	Triangles	Edges
Initial	4,078	7,846	11,924
Level 1	7,730	14,873	22,603
Level 2	14,036	27,062	41,098
Level 3	33,052	64,370	97,422
Level 4	67,967	133,232	201,199
Level 5	156,891	309,126	466,017
Level 6	314,857	623,033	937,890
Level 7	606,866	1,203,944	1,810,810

We ran our application from 1 to 64 nodes of the 64 node Linux PC cluster of the Real World Computing Partnership. Each node is equipped with a Pentium III 800 MHz processor and 512 MB memory and a Myrinet card. We used MPICH on top of the user-level communication library PM [15] that utilizes the Myrinet boards and uses a zero-copy protocol.

Table 2 shows the overall execution time in seconds for the solution of the Poisson problem. Note that our times include not only the times for the three refinement, partitioning, and remapping steps but also the computation of the element matrices, their assemblage and the execution of conjugate gradient methods on all levels. On a single processor we ran a completely sequential version of our program which of course needs no mapping algorithms at all and which contains no overhead from the parallelization.

Two different mesh partitioners were used to compute the new partition of the adaptively refined mesh, namely the graph partitioner ParMetis [8] (the ParMETIS_RepartMLRemap function) and our in-house development BHT (Balanced Hypersphere Tessellation) [2]. Figure 4 shows the different partitions of a mesh with BHT that correspond to two refinement steps. In our actual computations, we started with a finer subdivided mesh.

For the valuation of the results, one has to keep in mind that the application is highly irregular and dynamic. This table also indicates that for adaptively refined meshes, our

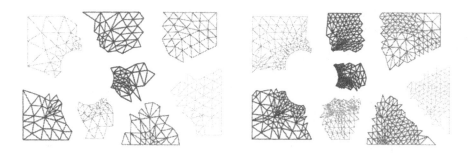

Fig. 4. Different steps of refinement (both domains are partitioned into 8 subdomains)

Table 2. Overall execution time of our adaptive finite element method

Nodes	1	2	4	8	16	32	64
BHT	121.7	78.5	39.6	20.4	10.8	6.8	7.5
ParMetis	121.7	83.2	41.8	21.6	11.8	7.4	6.3

coordinate-based partitioning algorithm (BHT) can compete with state-of-the-art graph partitioners. A further advantage of BHT is its low memory consumption.

5 Conclusions and Future Work

Janus provides a small yet very expressible set of concepts and template classes for the implementation of mesh based scientific applications. An important feature of Janus is its unified treatment of regular and irregular spatial structures. Two phase domains and relations make highly flexible yet slow classical data structures (trees, lists) dispensable for the implementation of irregular scientific problems. This makes it very attractive to use our library for the implementation of adaptive mesh methods.

The main components of Janus, i.e., its domain, relation, and domain function classes are very much application-oriented abstractions. As a consequence, the whole program development is raised to a higher level. Communication, for example, is expressed by *pull* and *push* operations of relation objects. Janus provides efficient implementations of these operations both for parallel and sequential platforms. Thus, these low-level aspects of scientific programming cease to be a problem for the application programmer.

Janus is not only used for the implementation of two-dimensional mesh methods. An important feature of Janus is that its abstractions are essentially dimension free. The Fracture Group at the Theory Center of Cornell University utilizes Janus to represent the mesh components of a three-dimensional finite element crack simulation. It has been shown in this project that Janus can interoperate with other libraries, since the linear systems are solved with PETSc after being constructed with Janus. To support this interoperability, we plan to develop a Janus interface to PETSc. We are also working on an implementation of Janus for shared memory systems on top of OpenMP. More information about Janus (including the source code) can be obtained from the web site http://www.first.gmd.de/janus.

References

1. S. Balay, W. D. Gropp, L. C. McInnes, and B. F. Smith. Efficient Management of Parallelism in Object-Oriented Numerical Software Libraries Programming. In A. M. Bruaset E. Arge and H. P. Langtangen, editors, *Modern Software Tools in Scientific Computing*, pages 163–202. Birkhauser Press, 1997.
2. M. Besch and H.W. Pohl. Topographic Data Mapping by Balanced Hypersphere Tesselation. In *Proceedings of Euro-Par Conference*, LNCS, Lyon, France, August 1996. Springer-Verlag.
3. Scott Cohn. *Home Page of SAMRAI: Structured Adaptive Mesh Refinement Applications Infrastructure*. Lawrence Livermore National Laboratory. http://www.llnl.gov/CASC/SAMRAI/team.html.
4. Peter Deuflhard. Cascadic conjugate gradient methods for elliptic partial differential equations. algorithm and numerical results. In D. Keyes and J. Xu, editors, *Proc. of the 7th Int. Conf. on Domain Decomposition Methods 1993*, pages 29–42, Providence, 1994. AMS.
5. J. Gerlach and P. Gottschling. Finite Elements with Janus. Technical Report in preparation, Real World Computing Partnership, Japan, 2000.
6. J. Gerlach, P. Gottschling, and H.W. Pohl. Core Components of Janus, Release 2.0. Technical Report TR D-00-028, Real World Computing Partnership, Japan, 2000.
7. S. Karmesin, J. Crotinger, J. Cummings, S. Haney, W. Humphrey, J. Reynders, S. Smith, and T.J. Williams. Array Design and Expression Evaluation in POOMA II. In *Proceedings of ISCOPE 98*, volume 1505 of *LNCS*, pages 231–238, Santa Fe, New Mexico, USA, December 1998. Springer-Verlag.
8. G. Karypis. *Metis a Family of Multilevel Partitioning Algorithms*. http://www-users.cs.umn.edu/˜karypis/metis/main.shtml.
9. L.-Q. Lee, J. Siek, and A. Lumsdaine. Generic Graph Algorithms for Sparse Matrix Ordering. In *Proc. of ISCOPE 99*, LNCS, San Francisco, December 1999. Springer-Verlag.
10. D.R. Musser and A.A. Stepanov. Generic Programming. In *First Int. Joint Conf. of ISSAC-88 and AAECC-6*, volume 358 of *LNCS*, pages 13–25. Springer, June 1988.
11. J. R. Shewchuk. *A Two-Dimensional Quality Mesh Generator and Delaunay Triangulator*. http://www.cs.cmu.edu/˜quake/triangle.html.
12. J. G. Siek and A. Lumsdaine. The Matrix Template Library: A Generic Programming Approach to High Performance Numerical Algebra. In *Proceedings of ISCOPE 98*, volume 1505 of *LNCS*, pages 59–70, Santa Fe, New Mexico, USA, December 1998. Springer-Verlag.
13. M. Snir, S. Otto, S. Huss-Ledermann, D. Walker, and J. Dongarra. *MPI—The Complete Reference, Volume 1, The MPI Core*. The MIT Press, 1998.
14. Alex Stepanov. Standard Template Library Programmer's Guide. http://www.sgi.com/Technology/STL.
15. Hiroshi Tezuka, Atsushi Hori, Yutaka Ishikawa, and Mitsuhisa Sato. PM: An Operating System Coordinated High Performance Communication Library. In Bob Hertzberger Peter Sloot, editor, *High-Performance Computing and Networking*, volume 1225 of *Lecture Notes in Computer Science*, pages 708–717. Springer, April 1997.

DSM-PM2: A Portable Implementation Platform for Multithread DSM Consistency Protocols

Gabriel Antoniu and Luc Bougé

LIP, ENS Lyon, 46 Allée d'Italie, 69364 Lyon Cedex 07, France
Contact: Gabriel.Antoniu@ens-lyon.fr

Abstract. DSM-PM2 is a platform for designing, implementing and experimenting with multithreaded DSM consistency protocols. It provides a generic toolbox which facilitates protocol design and allows for easy experimentation with alternative protocols for a given consistency model. DSM-PM2 is portable across a wide range of clusters. We illustrate its power with figures obtained for different protocols implementing sequential consistency, release consistency and Java consistency, on top of Myrinet, Fast-Ethernet and SCI clusters.

1 Introduction

In their traditional flavor, Distributed Shared Memory (DSM) libraries [15, 18, 19, 10] allow a number of separate processes to share a common address space using a *consistency protocol* according to a semantics specified by some given *consistency model*: sequential consistency, release consistency, etc. The processes may usually be physically distributed among a number of computing nodes interconnected through some communication library. The design of the DSM library is often highly dependent on the selected consistency model and on the communication library. Also, only a few of them are able to exploit the power of modern thread libraries to provide multithreaded protocols, or at least to provide thread-safe versions of the consistency protocols.

Most approaches to DSM programming assume that the DSM library and the underlying architecture are fixed, and that it is up to the programmer to fit his program with them. We think that such a *static* vision fails to appreciate the possibilities of this area of programming. We believe that a better approach is to provide the application programmer with an *implementation platform* where *both* the application *and* the multithreaded DSM consistency protocol can possibly be *co-designed* and tuned for performance. This aspect is crucial if the platform is used as target for a compiler: the implementation of the consistency model through a specific protocol can then directly benefit from the specific properties of the code, enforced by the compiler in the code generation process. The platform should moreover be *portable*, so that the programmers do not have to commit to some existing communication library or operating system, or at least be able to postpone this decision as late as possible.

DSM-PM2 is a prototype implementation platform for multithreaded DSM programming which attempts to meet these requirements. Its general structure and programming interface are presented in Section 2. Section 3 discusses in more detail how to select and define protocols. A given consistency model can be implemented via multiple alternative protocols. We give an overview of the implementation of several protocols for various consistency models, including sequential consistency, release consistency and Java consistency (which is a variant of release consistency). In particular, two alternative protocols addressing the sequential consistency model are described, a first one based on *page migration*, and the second one using *thread migration*, as enabled by the underlying multithreading library. Finally, we illustrate the portability and efficiency of DSM-PM2 by reporting performance measurements on top of different cluster architectures using various communication interfaces and interconnection networks: BIP [20]/Myrinet, TCP/Myrinet, TCP/FastEthernet, SISCI/SCI [9].

Related work

The concept of Distributed Shared Memory was proposed more than a decade ago [15]. Important efforts have been subsequently made to improve the performance of software DSM systems and many such systems were proposed to illustrate new ideas. Progresses related to the relaxation of consistency protocols were illustrated with Munin [6] (for release consistency), TreadMarks [1] (to study the impact of laziness in coherence propagation, through lazy release consistency), Midway [4] (for entry consistency), and Brazos [21] (for scope consistency). Recent software DSM systems, such as Millipede [11], CVM [13] and Brazos integrate the use of multithreading.

Our work is more closely related to that of DSM-Threads [16], a system which extends POSIX multithreading to distributed environments by providing a multithreaded DSM. Our approach is different essentially by the generic support and the ability to support *new*, user-defined consistency protocols. Millipede [11] also integrates threads with Distributed Shared Memory. It has been designed for a specific execution environment (Windows NT cluster with Myrinet) and focuses on sequential consistency only. CVM [13] is another software DSM system which provides multithreading (essentially to hide the network latency) and supports multiple consistency models and protocols. However, CVM's communication layer targets the UDP protocol only, whereas DSM-PM2 captures the benefits of PM2's portability on a large variety of communication interfaces: it is currently available on modern Myrinet and SCI high-performance clusters run with Linux. The primary goal of DSM-PM2 is to provide a portable platform for easy protocol experimentation. Its customizability makes it also valuable as a target for compilers as the Java Hyperion compiler discussed in Section 3.3.

2   DSM-PM2: an overview

2.1   The PM2 runtime system

PM2 (Parallel Multithreaded Machine) [17] is a multithreaded environment for distributed architectures. It provides a POSIX-like interface to create, manipulate and synchronize lightweight threads in user space, in a distributed environment. Its basic mechanism for inter-node interaction is the *Remote Procedure Call* (RPC). Using RPCs, the PM2 threads can invoke the remote execution of user-defined *services*. Such invocations can either be handled by a pre-existing thread, or they can involve the creation of a new thread. While threads running on the same node can freely share data, PM2 threads running on distant nodes may only interact through RPC. This mechanism can be used either to send/retrieve information to/from the remote node, or to have some remote action executed. The minimal latency of a RPC is 6 μs over SISCI/SCI and 8 μs over BIP/Myrinet on our local Linux clusters.

PM2 includes two main components. For multithreading, it uses Marcel, an efficient, user-level, POSIX-like thread package. To ensure network portability, PM2 uses an efficient communication library called Madeleine [5], which was ported across a wide range of communication interfaces, including high-performance ones such as BIP [20], SISCI, VIA [7], as well as more traditional ones such as TCP, and MPI.

An interesting feature of PM2 is its *thread migration* mechanism that allows threads to be transparently and preemptively moved from one node to another during their execution. Such a functionality is typically useful to implement generic policies for dynamic load balancing, independently of the applications: the load of each processing node can be evaluated according to some measure, and balanced using preemptive migration. The key feature enabling preemptiveness is the *iso-address* approach to dynamic allocation featured by PM2. The isomalloc allocation routine guarantees that the range of virtual addresses allocated by a thread on a node will be left free on any other node. Thus, threads can be safely migrated across nodes: their stacks and their dynamically allocated data are just copied on the destination node at the *same* virtual address as on the original node. This guarantees the validity of all pointers without any further restriction [3]. Migrating a thread with a minimal stack and no attached data, takes 62 μs over SISCI/SCI and 75 μs over BIP/Myrinet on our local Linux clusters.

2.2 DSM-PM2: towards a portable implementation platform

DSM-PM2 provides the illusion of a common address space shared by all PM2 threads irrespective of their location and thus implements the concept of Distributed Shared Memory on top of the distributed architecture of PM2. But DSM-PM2 is not simply *a* DSM layer for PM2: its goal is to provide a portable implementation platform for multithreaded DSM consistency protocols. Given that all DSM communication primitives have been implemented using PM2's RPC mechanism based on Madeleine, DSM-PM2 inherits PM2's wide network portability. However, the most important feature of DSM-PM2 is its *customizability*: actually, the main design goal was to provide support for implementing, tuning and comparing several consistency models, and alternative protocols for a given consistency model.

As a starting remark, we can notice that all DSM systems share a number of common features. Every DSM system, aimed for instance at illustrating a new version of some protocol, has to implement again a number of core functionalities. It is therefore interesting to ask: What are the features that need to be present in *any* DSM system? And then: What are the features that are specific to a *particular* DSM system? By answering these questions, we become able to build a system where the core mechanisms shared by the existing DSM systems are provided as a *generic*, common layer, on top of which specific protocols can be easily built. In our study, we limit ourselves to *page-based* DSM systems.

Access detection. Most DSM systems use page faults to detect accesses to shared data, in order to carry out actions necessary to guarantee consistency. The generic core should provide routines to detect page faults, to extract information related to each fault (address, fault type, etc.) and to associate protocol-specific consistency actions to a page-fault event.

Page manager. Page-based DSM systems use a page table which stores information about the shared pages. Each memory page is handled individually. Some information fields are common to virtually all protocols: local access rights, current owner, etc. Other fields may be specific to some protocol. The generic core should provide the page table structure and a basic set of functions to manipulate page entries. Also, the page table structure should be designed so that new information fields could be added, as needed by the protocols of interest.

DSM communication. We can notice that the known DSM protocols use a limited set of communication routines, like sending a page request, sending a page, sending diffs (for some protocols implementing weak consistency models, like release consistency). Such a set of routines should also be part of the generic core.

Synchronization and consistency. Weaker consistency models, like release, entry, or scope consistency require that consistency actions be taken at synchronization points. In order to support these models, the generic core should provide synchronization objects (locks, barriers, etc.) and enable consistency actions to be associated to synchronization events.

Thread-safety. Modern environments for parallel programming use multithreading. All the data structures and management routines provided by the generic core should be *thread-safe*: multiple concurrent threads should be able to safely call these routines.

A closer study of page-based consistency protocols enables to list up a small number of events which should trigger consistency actions: page faults, receipt of a page request, receipt of the requested page, receipt of an invalidation request. Additionally, for weak consistency models, lock acquire, lock release and barrier calls are events to be associated with consistency actions. In the current version of DSM-PM2, there are 8 actions. The detailed list is given in Table 1.

Protocol function	Description
read_fault_handler	Called on a read page fault
write_fault_handler	Called on a write page fault
read_server	Called on receiving a request for read access
write_server	Called on receiving a request for write access
invalidate_server	Called on receiving a request for invalidation
receive_page_server	Called on receiving a page
lock_acquire	Called after having acquired a lock
lock_release	Called before releasing a lock

Table 1. DSM-PM2 protocol actions.

Once the generic core has been delineated, we can consider building consistency protocols on top of it. Designing a protocol in DSM-PM2 consists in providing a set of 8 routines, one for each action identified above. These routines are designed using on the API of the generic components. They are automatically called by DSM-PM2, and nothing more has to be done by the programmer. According to our personal experience, the code for the routines is quite manageable: a few hundreds of lines for the whole set of routines of a typical protocol. A key feature of DSM-PM2 is that all the mechanisms provided by the generic core are *thread-safe*. The task of the protocol designer is thus considerably alleviated as most (if not all!) subtle synchronization problems are already addressed by the core routines.

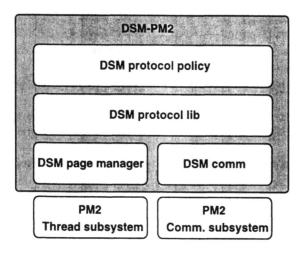

Fig. 1. Overview of the DSM-PM2 software architecture.

As a consequence of our distinction between generic core mechanisms and protocol-specific actions, DSM-PM2 is structured in layers (Figure 1). At the lowest level, DSM-PM2 includes two main components which make up the the main part of the generic core: the *DSM page manager* and the *DSM communication module*. Both are based on the API of PM2: no direct access to the thread low-level structures and to the underlying communication library are made.

The *DSM page manager* is essentially dedicated to the low-level management of memory pages. It implements a distributed table containing page ownership information and maintains the appropriate access rights on each node. This table has been designed to be generic enough so that it could be exploited to implement protocols which need a fixed page manager, as well as protocols based on a dynamic page manager (see [15] for a classification of page managers). Of course, each protocol uses the fields in the page entries of the table as required by its corresponding page management strategy (which is decided at the higher, *protocol library* level). Consequently, a field may have different semantics in different protocols and may be even left unused by some protocols. Also, new fields could be easily added if needed in the future.

The *DSM communication module* is responsible for providing elementary communication mechanisms, such as delivering requests for page copies, sending pages, invalidating pages or sending diffs. This module is implemented using PM2's RPC mechanism, which turns out to be well-suited for this kind of task. For instance, requesting a copy of a remote page for read access can essentially be seen as invoking a remote service. On the other hand, since the RPCs are implemented on top of the Madeleine communication library, the DSM-PM2 communication module is portable across all communication interfaces supported by Madeleine at no extra cost.

The routines which compose a protocol are defined using a toolbox called the *DSM protocol library* layer. It provides routines to perform elementary actions such as bringing a copy of a remote page to a thread, migrating a thread to some remote data, invalidating all copies of a page, etc. All the available routines are thread-safe. This library is built on top of the two base components of the generic core: the *DSM page manager* and the *DSM communication module*.

Finally, at the highest level, a *DSM protocol policy* layer is responsible for building consistency protocols out of a subset of the available library routines. An arbitrary number of protocols can be defined at this level, which may be selected by the application through a specific library call. Some *classical* protocols are already built-in, as summarized in Table 2, but the user can also add new protocols, as described in Section 2.3 by defining each of the component routines of each protocol and by registering it using specific library calls.

2.3 Using protocols

Protocol	Consistency	Basic features
li_hudak	Sequential	MRSW protocol. Page replication on read access, page migration on write access. Dynamic distributed manager.
migrate_thread	Sequential	Uses thread migration on both read and write faults. Fixed distributed manager.
erc_sw	Release	MRSW protocol implementing *eager* release consistency. Dynamic distributed manager.
hbrc_mw	Release	MRMW protocol implementing *home-based lazy* release consistency. Fixed distributed manager. Uses twins and on-release diffing.
java_ic	Java	Home-based MRMW protocol, based on explicit *inline checks* (ic)for locality. Fixed distributed manager. Uses on-the-fly diff recording.
java_pf	Java	Home-based MRMW protocol, based on on *page faults*(pf). Fixed distributed manager. Uses on-the-fly diff recording.

Table 2. Consistency protocols currently available in the DSM-PM2 library.

```
#include "pm2.h"

BEGIN_DSM_DATA
int x = 34;
/* ... */
END_DSM_DATA

void main (void)
{
  /* Use the built-in 'li_hudak' protocol */

  pm2_dsm_set_default_protocol(li_hudak);
  pm2_init();

  x++;

  /* ... */
}
```

Fig. 2. Using DSM-PM2 with a built-in protocol.

In DSM-PM2, a specific protocol is a set of actions designed to guarantee consistency according to a consistency model. In our current implementation, a protocol is specified through 8 routines (listed in Table 1) that are automatically called by the generic DSM support as needed. Each protocol is labeled by a unique identifier. This identifier can for instance be used to set it up as the default protocol or to associate it to dynamically allocated shared objects. DSM-PM2 protocols can be specified and used in three different ways.

Using built-in protocols. The easiest way consists in selecting one of the available built-in protocols. In its current stage of development, DSM-PM2 provides 6 such protocols, whose main characteristics are summarized in Table 2 and detailed in Section 3. On Figure 2, the li_hudak protocol is declared as the default protocol for the static shared area.

Building new protocols. The user can also a define a new protocol by providing each of its component routines and by registering it using a specific library call. The newly created protocol can then be used exactly in the same way as built-in protocols.

```
int new_proto;
new_prot = dsm_create_protocol
  (read_fault_handler, write_fault_handler,
   read_server, write_server,
   invalidate_server, receive_page_server,
   acquire_handler, release_handler);

pm2_dsm_set_default_protocol(proto);
```

Building protocols using library routines A mixed approach consists in using *existing* library routines, as provided in the *DSM protocol library* layer, rather than new, user-defined routines, but combine then in some ad-hoc way. One may thus consider *hybrid* approaches such as page replication on read fault (like in the li_hudak protocol) and thread migration on write fault (like in the migrate_thread protocol). One may even embed a dynamic mechanism selection within the protocol, switching for instance from page migration to thread migration depending on ad-hoc criteria. However, the user is responsible for using these features in a consistent way to produce a valid protocol.

Observe that no pre-processing of the code file is used. Consequently, it is possible to define a number of protocols in a program and to dynamically select one of them according to the arguments provided by the user without any recompilation:

```
int proto1, proto2;
proto1 = dsm_create_protocol(...);
proto2 = dsm_create_protocol(...);

if (...)  pm2_dsm_set_default_protocol(proto1);
else pm2_dsm_set_default_protocol(proto2);
```

Again, the built-in protocols are just pre-defined protocols, so they can freely be included in such a selection.

On Figure 2, a protocol is associated to a static memory area. DSM-PM2 also provides dynamic allocation for shared memory. Each such dynamically-allocated shared area can be managed with a specific protocol, which can be specified through its creation attribute as illustrated. (Otherwise, the default protocol set by pm2_dsm_set_default_protocol is used.) Consequently, different DSM protocols may be associated to different DSM memory areas within the same application.

```
#define N 128
int *ptr;
dsm_attr_t attr;

dsm_attr_set_protocol(&attr, li_hudak);
ptr = (int*)dsm_malloc(N*sizeof(int),&attr);
```

In the current version of the system, DSM-PM2 does not provide any specific support to dynamically *switch* the management of a memory area from one protocol to another one within the same run. However, this can be achieved if needed through a careful synchronization at the program level (e.g. through barriers). Essentially, one has to keep the corresponding memory area from being accessed by the application threads during the protocol switch, since this operation involves modifications in the distributed page table on all nodes.

DSM-PM2 provides a multithreaded DSM interface: static and dynamic data can be shared by all the threads in the system. Since the programming interface is intended both for direct use and as a target for compilers, no pre-processing is assumed in the general case and accesses to shared data are detected using page faults. Nevertheless, when DSM-PM2 is used as a compiler target, accesses to shared data may be carried out through specific runtime primitives like get and put (and not through direct assignment). The implementation of these primitives may then explicitly check for data locality and handle consistency accordingly. DSM-PM2 thus provides a way to bypass the page fault detection and to directly activate the protocol actions.

3 Built-in protocols available with DSM-PM2

Currently, DSM-PM2 provides 6 built-in protocols, whose main characteristics are summarized in Table 2. All these protocols share two important common features. 1) Their implementations are *multithreaded*: it uses multiple "hidden" threads to maintain the internal data structures and to enhance reactivity to external events such as message arrival. 2) They are *thread-safe*: an arbitrary number of user-level threads can concurrently access pages on any node and threads on the same node safely share the same page copy. These distinctive features required that the traditional consistency protocols (usually written for single-threaded systems) which we used as a starting point be adapted to a multi-threaded context to handle thread-level concurrency. As opposed to the traditional protocols where all page faults on a node are processed sequentially, concurrent requests may be processed in parallel in a multithreaded context, should they concern the same page or different pages.

3.1 Sequential consistency

We provide two protocols for sequential consistency. The li_hudak protocol relies on a variant of the dynamic distributed manager MRSW (multiple reader, single writer) algorithm described by Li and Hudak [15], adapted by Mueller [16]. It uses page replication on read fault and page migration on write fault. Note that in a multithreaded context, the *single* writer refers to a node, not to a thread, since all the threads on the 'writer' node share the same copy. They may thus write it concurrently.

Alternatively, DSM-PM2 provides a new protocol for sequential consistency based on thread migration (migrate_thread), illustrated in Figure 3. When a thread accesses a page and does not have the appropriate access rights, it executes the page fault handler which simply migrates the thread to the node owning the page (as specified by the local page table). On reaching the destination node, the thread exits the handler and repeats the access, which is now successfully carried out and the thread continues its execution. Note the simplicity of this protocol, which essentially relies on a single function: the thread migration primitive provided by PM2. The counterpart is that the pages are not replicated in this protocol (i.e., for each page, there is a unique node where the page can be accessed both for read and write), so that all threads accessing a non local page will migrate to the corresponding owning node. Though the migration cost is generally very low, the efficiency of this protocol is highly influenced by the distribution of the shared data, which has a direct impact on the load balancing (since the threads migrate to the data they access). This point is discussed in Section 4.

The protocol described above crucially depends on an *iso-address* approach to data allocation [3]: not only static, but also dynamically allocated DSM pages are mapped at the *same* virtual address on all nodes, using the isomalloc allocation routine of PM2.

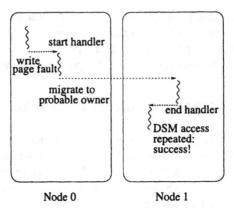

Fig. 3. Sequential consistency using thread migration: on page fault, the thread migrates to the node where the data is located.

On exiting the fault handler after migration, the thread automatically repeats the access at the *same* address, which does correspond to the same piece of data.

3.2 Release consistency

DSM-PM2 also provides two alternative implementations for release consistency. The erc_sw protocol is a MRSW protocol for eager release consistency. It uses page replication on read fault and page migration on write fault, based on the same dynamic distributed manager scheme as li_hudak. Page ownership migrates along with the write access rights. Pages in the copyset get invalidated on lock release.

Alternatively, the hbrc_mw protocol is a home-based protocol allowing multiple writers (MRMW protocol) by using the 'classical' twinning technique described in [14]. Essentially, each page has a home node, where all threads have write access. On page fault, a copy of the page is brought from the home node and a twin copy gets created. On release, page diffs are computed and sent to the home node, which subsequently invalidates third-party writer nodes. On receiving such an invalidation, these latter nodes need to compute and send their own diffs (if any) to the home node.

3.3 Java consistency

DSM-PM2 provides two protocols which directly implement consistency as specified by the Java Memory Model [12] (we refer to this consistency using the term "Java consistency"). Thanks to these protocols, DSM-PM2 is currently used by the Hyperion Java compiling system [2] and consequently supports the execution of compiled threaded Java programs on clusters. Our DSM-PM2 protocols were co-designed with Hyperion's memory module and this approach enabled us to make aggressive optimizations using information from the upper layers. For instance, a number of synchronizations could thereby be optimized out.

The Java Memory Model allows threads to keep locally cached copies of objects. Consistency is provided by requiring that a thread's object cache be flushed upon entry to a monitor and that local modifications made to cached objects be transmitted to the central memory when a thread exits a monitor. Gontmakher and Schuster [8] have shown that the JMM provides Release Consistency for synchronized access to non-volatile variables and stricter forms of consistency for the other cases. That is, Java Consistency is equivalent to Release Consistency in most cases.

The concept of *main memory* is implemented with DSM-PM2 via a *home-based* approach. The home node is in charge of managing the reference copy. Objects (initially stored on their home nodes) are replicated if accessed on other nodes. Note that at most one copy of an object may exist on a node and this copy is shared by all the threads running on that node. Thus, we avoid wasting memory by associating caches to nodes rather than to threads.

Since Hyperion uses specific access primitives to shared data (get and put), we can use explicit checks to detect if an object is present (i.e., has a copy) on the local node, thus by-passing the page-fault mechanism. If the object is present, it is directly accessed, else the page containing the object is brought to the local cache. This scheme is used by the java_ic protocol (where ic stands for inline check). Alternatively the java_pf protocol uses page faults to detect accesses to non-local objects (hence the pf suffix). Through the put access primitives, the modifications can be recorded at the moment when they are carried out, with object-field granularity. All local modifications are sent to the home node of the page by the main memory update primitive, called by the Hyperion run-time on exiting a monitor.

4 Performance evaluation

We present the raw performance of our basic protocol primitives on four different platforms. The measurements were first carried out on a cluster of 450 MHz PII nodes running Linux 2.2.13 interconnected by a Myrinet network using the BIP and TCP protocols and by a Fast Ethernet network under TCP. Then, the same measurements were realized on a cluster of PII 450 MHz nodes interconnected by a SCI network.

Table 3 reports the time (in μs) taken by each step involved when a read fault occurs on a node, assuming that the corresponding protocol is *page-transfer* based (which is the case for all built-in protocols, except for migrate_thread). First, the faulting instruction leads to a signal (*page fault*), which is caught by a handler that inspects the page table to locate the page owner and then requests the page to this owner (request page). The request is processed on the owner node and the required page is sent to the requester (*page transfer*). The time reported here corresponds to a common 4 kB page. Finally, the *protocol overhead* includes the request processing time on the owner node and the page installation on the requesting node.

As one can observe, the protocol overhead of DSM-PM2 is only up to 15% of the total access time, as most of the time is spent with communication. The *protocol overhead* essentially consists in updating page table information and setting the appropriate access rights.

Operation	BIP/Myrinet	TCP/Myrinet	TCP/Fast Ethernet	SISCI/SCI
Page fault	11	11	11	11
Request page	23	220	220	38
Page transfer	138	343	736	119
Protocol overhead	26	26	26	26
Total (μs)	**198**	**600**	**993**	**194**

Table 3. Processing a read-fault under page-migration policy: Performance analysis.

In Table 4 we report the cost (in μs) for processing a read fault assuming a *thread-migration* based implementation of the consistency protocol. The *protocol overhead* is here insignificant (less than 1 μs), since it merely consists of a call to the underlying run-time to migrate the thread to the owner node. In PM2, migrating a thread means moving the thread stack and the thread descriptor to the destination node, possibly together with some private dynamically allocated data (which is not the case in this example).

Operation	BIP/Myrinet	TCP/Myrinet	TCP/Fast Ethernet	SISCI/SCI
Page fault	11	11	11	11
Thread migration	75	280	373	62
Protocol overhead	1	1	1	1
Total (μs)	**87**	**292**	**385**	**74**

Table 4. Processing a read-fault under thread-migration policy: Performance analysis.

We can observe that this migration-based implementation outperforms the previous one, because thread migration is very efficient. Note however, that this migration time is closely related to the stack size of the thread. In our test program, the thread's stack was very small (about 1 kB), which is typically the case in many applications, but not in all applications. Thus, choosing between the implementation based on page transfer and the one based on thread migration deserves careful attention. Moreover, it may depend on other criteria such as the number and the location of the threads accessing the same page, and may be closely related to the load balance, as illustrated below. This is a research topic we plan to investigate in the future.

To illustrate DSM-PM2's ability to serve as an experimental platform for comparing consistency protocols, we have run a program solving the *Traveling Salesman Problem* for 14 randomly placed cities, using one application thread per node. Figure 4 presents run times for our 4 protocols implementing sequential and release consistency, on the BIP/Myrinet platform. Given that the only shared variable intensively accessed in this program is the current shortest path and that the accesses to this variable are always lock protected, the benefits of release consistency over sequential consistency are not illustrated here. But we can still remark that all protocols based on page migration perform better than the protocol using thread migration. This is essentially due to the fact that all computing threads migrate to the node holding the shared variable, which thus

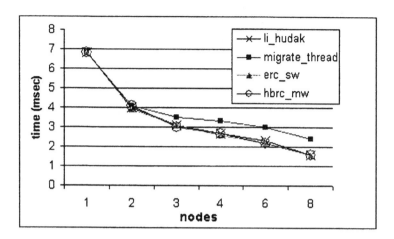

Fig. 4. Solving TSP for 14 cities with random inter-city distances: Comparison of 4 DSM protocols.

gets overloaded. We could expect a better behavior for this protocol with applications where shared data are evenly distributed across nodes and uniformly accessed.

To compare our two protocols for Java consistency, we have run a multithreaded Java program implementing a branch-and-bound solution to the minimal-cost map-coloring problem, compiled with Hyperion [2]. The program was run on a four-node cluster of 450 MHz Pentium II processors running Linux 2.2.13, interconnected by a SCI network using the SISCI API and solves the problem of coloring the twenty-nine eastern-most states in the USA using four colors with different costs. Figure 5 clearly shows that the protocol using access detection based on page faults (java_pf) outperforms the protocol based on in-line checks for locality (java_ic). This is due to the intensive use of objects in the program: remember that every get and put operation involves a check for locality in java_ic, whereas this is not the case for accesses to local objects when using java_pf. The overhead of fault handling appears to be significantly less important than the overhead due to checks, also thanks to a good distribution of the objects: local objects are intensively used, remote accesses (generating faults for java_pf) are not very frequent.

Of course, we are aware that the performance evaluation reported above can only be considered as preliminary. A more complete analysis is necessary to study the behavior of the DSM-PM2 protocols with respect to different classes of applications illustrating various sharing patterns, access patterns, synchronization methods, etc. This is part of our current work.

Finally, we can mention that very precise post-mortem monitoring tools are available in the PM2 platform, providing the user with valuable information on the time spent within each elementary function. This feature proves very helpful for understanding and improving protocol performance.

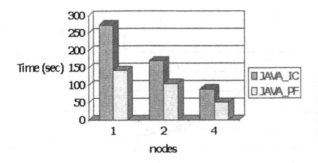

Fig. 5. Comparing the two protocols for Java consistency: page faults vs. in-line checks.

5 Conclusion

DSM-PM2 is a platform for designing, implementing and experimenting with multi-threaded DSM consistency protocols. It provides a generic toolbox which facilitates protocol design and allows for experimentation with alternative protocols for a given consistency model. DSM-PM2 is portable across a wide range of cluster architectures, using high-performance interconnection networks such as BIP/Myrinet, SISCI/SCI, VIA, as well as more traditional ones such as TCP, and MPI. In this paper, we have illustrated its power by presenting different protocols implementing sequential consistency, release consistency and Java consistency, on top of different cluster architectures: BIP/Myrinet, TCP/Myrinet, TCP/FastEthernet, SISCI/SCI.

DSM-PM2 is *not* just yet another multithreaded DSM library. It is aimed at exploring a new research direction, namely providing the designers of such protocols with *portable platforms* to experiment with alternative designs, in a generic, customizable environment, while providing tools for performance profiling, such as post-mortem analysis. We are convinced that many interesting ideas in DSM protocols could be more easily experimented using such *an open platform*: implementing everything from scratch is simply too hard! Also, such a platform enables *competing protocol designers* to compare their protocols within a common environment, using common profiling tools. Switching from one protocol to another, or switching from one communication library to another, can be done without changing anything to the application. No re-compiling is even needed if all the necessary routines have been linked beforehand. Finally, such a platform opens a large access to the area of *co-design*: indeed, the application and the protocol can then be designed and optimized *together*, instead of simply tuning the application on top of a fixed, existing protocol. This idea seems of particular interest in the case of compilers targeting DSM libraries, as demonstrated by the Hyperion Java compiler project reported above.

Currently, DSM-PM2 is operational on Linux 2.2.x and Solaris 6 or later. Extensive testing has been done on top of SISCI/SCI, TCP/Myrinet and BIP/Myrinet. All the protocols mentioned in Table 2 are available and hybrid protocols mixing thread migration and page replication can also be built out of library functions. We are currently working on a more thorough performance evaluation using the SPLASH-2 [22] benchmarks, which will be helpful to guide an efficient protocol use in applications.

Acknowledgments

We are grateful to Frank Mueller for his helpful explanations about the design of the DSM-Threads system. We thank Phil Hatcher for our fruitful collaboration on Java consistency. Last but not least, we thank Vincent Bernardi for his help with the design and implementation of the two protocols for release consistency within DSM-PM2.

References

1. C. Amza, A. L. Cox, S. Dwarkadas, P. Keleher, H. Lu, R. Rajamony, W. Yu, and W. Zwaenepoel. TreadMarks: Shared memory computing on networks of workstations. *IEEE Computer*, 29(2):18–28, February 1996.
2. G. Antoniu, L. Bougé, P. Hatcher, M. MacBeth, K. McGuigan, and R. Namyst. Compiling multithreaded Java bytecode for distributed execution. In *Euro-Par 2000: Parallel Processing*, volume 1900 of *Lect. Notes in Comp. Science*, pages 1039–1052, Munchen, Germany, August 2000. Springer-Verlag.
3. G. Antoniu, L. Bougé, and R. Namyst. An efficient and transparent thread migration scheme in the PM2 runtime system. In *Proc. 3rd Workshop on Runtime Systems for Parallel Programming (RTSPP '99)*, volume 1586 of *Lect. Notes in Comp. Science*, pages 496–510, San Juan, Puerto Rico, April 1999. Springer-Verlag.
4. B.N. Bershad, M.J. Zekauskas, and W.A. Sawdon. The Midway distributed shared memory system. In *Proc. of the 38th IEEE Int'l Computer Conf. (COMPCON Spring'93)*, pages 528–537, February 1993.
5. L. Bougé, J.-F. Méhaut, and R. Namyst. Efficient communications in multithreaded runtime systems. In *Proc. 3rd Workshop on Runtime Systems for Parallel Programming (RTSPP '99)*, volume 1586 of *Lect. Notes in Comp. Science*, pages 468–482, San Juan, Puerto Rico, April 1999. Springer-Verlag.
6. J. B. Carter. Design of the Munin distributed shared memory system. *Journal of Parallel and Distributed Computing*, 29:219–227, 1995. Special issue on distributed shared memory.
7. Dave Dunning, Greg Regnier, Gary McAlpine, Don Cameron, Bill Shubert, Frank Berry, Anne-Marie Merritt, Ed Gronke, and Chris Dodd. The Virtual Interface Architecture. *IEEE Micro*, pages 66–75, March 1998.
8. A. Gontmakher and A. Schuster. Java consistency: Non-operational characterizatons for Java memory behavior. In *Proc. of the Workshop on Java for High-Performance Computing*, Rhodes, June 1999.
9. IEEE. *Standard for Scalable Coherent Interface (SCI)*, August 1993. Standard no. 1596.
10. L. Iftode and J. P. Singh. Shared virtual memory: Progress and challenges. *Proceedings of the IEEE*, 87(3), March 1999.
11. A. Itzkovitz, A. Schuster, and L. Shalev. Thread migration and its application in distributed shared memory systems. *J. Systems and Software*, 42(1):71–87, July 1998.
12. B. Joy, G. Steele, J. Gosling, and G. Bracha. *The Java language specification*. Addison Wesley, Second edition, 2000.
13. P. Keleher. The relative importance of concurrent writers and weak consistency models. In *16th Intl. Conf. on Distributed Computing Systems*, Hong Kong, May 1998.

14. P. Keleher, A.L.Cox, S. Dwarkadas, and W. Zwaenepoel. An evaluation of software based release consistent protocols. *J. Parallel and Distrib. Comp.*, 26(2):126–141, September 1995.

15. K. Li and P. Hudak. Memory coherence in shared virtual memory systems. *ACM Transactions on Computer Systems*, 7(4):321–359, November 1989.

16. F. Mueller. Distributed shared-memory threads: DSM-Threads. In *Proc. Workshop on Run-Time Systems for Parallel Programming (RTSPP)*, pages 31–40, Geneva, Switzerland, April 1997.

17. R. Namyst. *PM2: an environment for a portable design and an efficient execution of irregular parallel applications*. PhD thesis, Univ. Lille 1, France, January 1997. In French.

18. B. Nitzberg and V. Lo. Distributed shared memory: A survey of issues and algorithms. *IEEE computer*, 24(8):52–60, September 1991.

19. J. Protic, M. Tomasevic, and V. Milutinovic. Distributed shared memory: concepts and systems. *IEEE Paralel and Distributed Technology*, pages 63–79, 1996.

20. Loïc Prylli and Bernard Tourancheau. BIP: a new protocol designed for high performance networking on Myrinet. In *1st Workshop on Personal Computer based Networks Of Workstations (PC-NOW '98)*, volume 1388 of *Lect. Notes in Comp. Science*, pages 472–485. Springer-Verlag, April 1998.

21. E. Speight and J.K. Bennett. Brazos: A third generation DSM system. In *Proc. of the USENIX Windows/NT Workshop*, pages 95–106, August 1997.

22. S. C. Woo, M. Ohara, E. Torrie, J.P. Singh, and A. Gupta. The SPLASH-2 programs: Characterization and methodological considerations. In *Proc. 2nd Annual Int'l Symp. on Comp. Arch.*, pages 24–36, Santa Margherita Ligure, Italy, June 1995.

Implementation of a Skeleton-Based Parallel Programming Environment Supporting Arbitrary Nesting

Rémi Coudarcher, Jocelyn Sérot, and Jean-Pierre Dérutin

LASMEA
UMR 6602 UBP/CNRS
Université Blaise-Pascal - Clermont II
Campus universitaire des Cézeaux - 24 avenue des Landais - F-63177 AUBIERE Cedex
FRANCE
`Remi.Coudarcher@lasmea.univ-bpclermont.fr`

Abstract. This paper presents the latest version of the SKiPPER skeleton-based parallel programming environment dedicated to fast prototyping of vision applications. Compared to the previous version, its main innovative feature is the ability to handle arbitrary skeleton *nesting*.

1 Introduction

The goal of the SKiPPER project is to develop a parallel programming methodology allowing fast prototyping of vision applications on embedded and/or dedicated parallel platforms. This methodology should allow field application programmers – as opposed to parallel programming specialists – to build parallel vision applications easily while preserving efficiency.

The SKiPPER-I suite of tools, described for instance in [9] [10] [20], was the first instantiation of this methodology. It is however limited in terms of skeleton composition. In particular, it cannot accommodate arbitrary skeleton nesting. The SKiPPER-II implementation described in this paper is an attempt to solve this problem.

The paper is organised as follows. Section 2 briefly recalls the skeleton-based parallel programming concepts in general and their incarnation in SKiPPER-I in particular. Section 3 is a presentation of the concepts and techniques used in SKiPPER-II. Section 4 gives some (very preliminary) results. Section 5 is a short review of related work on skeleton nesting. And finally section 6 concludes the paper.

2 Skeleton-based parallel programming and SKiPPER-I

Skeleton-based parallel programming methodologies [4] [5] provide a way for conciliating fast prototyping and efficiency. They aim at providing user guidance and a mostly automatic procedure for designing and implementing parallel applications. For that purpose, they provide a set of *algorithmic skeletons*, which are *higher-order program constructs encapsulating common and recurrent forms of parallelism* to make them readily available for the application programmer. The latter does not need to take into account low-level implementation details such as task partitioning and mapping, data distribution, communication scheduling and load-balancing. The overall result is a significant reduction of the design-implement-validate cycle time – especially on dedicated parallel platforms.

Due to our interest in image processing, we have designed and implemented a skeleton-based parallel programming environment, called SKiPPER, based on a set of skeletons specifically designed for parallel vision applications [9] [10] [20] [17]. This library of skeletons was designed from a retrospective analysis of existing parallel code. It includes four skeletons:

- SCM, Split-Compute-Merge skeleton,

- DF, Data Farming,

- TF, Task Farming (a recursive version of the DF skeleton),

- ITERMEM, Iteration with Memory,

The SCM skeleton is devoted to regular, "geometric" processing of iconic data, in which the input image is split into a fixed number of sub-images, each sub-image is processed independently and the final result is obtained by merging the results computed on sub-image (the sub-images may overlap and do not systematically cover the entire input image). This skeleton is applicable whenever the number of sub-images is fixed and the amount of work on each sub-image is the same, resulting in an very even work-load. Typical examples include convolutions, median-filtering and histogram computation.

The DF skeleton is a generic harness for so-called process farms. A process farm is a widely used construct for data-parallelism in which a farmer process has access to a pool of worker processes, each of them computing the *same* function. The farmer distributes items from an input list to workers and collects results back. The effect is to apply the function to every data item. We use a variant of this scheme in which the results collected by the farmer are accumulated using a specific user function instead of being just added to an output list. The DF skeleton shows its utility when the application requires the processing of irregular data, for instance an arbitrary list of windows of different sizes. In this case, a static allocation of computing processes to processors (like with the SCM skeleton) is not always possible and would result, anyway, to an uneven work-load between processors (which in turn results in a poor efficiency). The DF skeleton handles this situation by having the farmer process directly doling out computing processes allocation to worker processes. Typically, the farmer starts by sending a packet to each worker, then waits for a result from a worker and immediately send another packet to him. This until no packets are left and the workers are no longer processing data. Each worker, on the other side, simply waits for a packet, processes it and returns the result to the farmer until it receives a stop condition from the farmer. This technique gives an inherent, primitive load-balancing. It is only efficient, however, if there are more data items than processors.

The TF skeleton may be viewed as a generalisation of the DF one, in which the processing of one data item by a worker may recursively generate new items to be processed. These data items are then returned to the farmer to be added to a queue from which tasks are doled out (hence the name *task farming*). A typical application of the TF skeleton is image segmentation using classical recursive divide-and-conquer algorithms.

The ITERMEM skeleton does not properly speaking encapsulate parallel behaviour, but is used whenever the *iterative* nature of the real-time vision algorithms, *i.e.* the fact that they do not process single images but continuous *streams* of images, has to be made explicit. A typical situation is when computations on the nth image depend on results computed on the n-1th (or n-k^{th}). Such "feedback" patterns are very common in tracking algorithms for instance, where a model of the system state is used to predict the position of the tracked objects in the next image. Another example is motion detection by frame-to-frame difference. The ITERMEM skeleton will always be the "top-level" skeleton, taking as parameter either a sequential function or a composition of other skeletons. The latter case is the only situation in which SKiPPER-I supports nested skeletons.

Using SKiPPER, the application designer:

- provides the source code of the sequential application-specific functions,
- describes the parallel structure of his application in terms of composition of skeleton chosen in the library.

This description is made by using a subset of the CAML functional language, as shown on the Figure 1 where a SCM skeleton is used to express the parallel computation of an histogram using a geometric partitioning of the input image. On this figure, row_partition, seq_histo, merge_histo and display_histo are the application-specific sequential functions (written in C) and scm is the above mentioned skeleton. This CAML program is the so-called *skeletal program specification*. In SKiPPER-I, it is turned into executable code by first translating it into a graph of parametric process templates and then mapping this graph onto the target architecture.

```
let img      = read_img     512 512 ;;
let histo    = scm          8   row_partition seq_histo merge_histo img ;;
let main     = display_histo img histo ;;
```

Fig. 1. A "skeletal" program in CAML.

Completely designed by the end of 1998, SKiPPER-I has already been used for implementing several realistic parallel vision applications, such as connected component labelling [10], vehicle tracking [20] and road tracking/reconstruction [19].

But the current version of SKiPPER does not support *skeleton nesting, i.e.* the ability for a skeleton to take another skeleton as argument. Arbitrary skeleton nesting raises challenging implementation issues as evidenced in [16], [13], [12] or [14] (see section 5). This paper specifically deals with these issues by presenting a new implementation of the SKiPPER parallel programming environment (referred to as SKiPPER-II in the sequel) supporting arbitrary nesting of skeletons. This implementation is based on a completely revised execution model for skeletons. Its three main features are:

- the reformulation of all skeletons as instances of a very general one: a new version of the Task Farming skeleton (called TF/II),
- a fully dynamic scheduling mechanism (scheduling was mainly static in SKiPPER-I),
- a portable implementation of skeletons based on a *MPI* communication layer.

3 SKiPPER-II

One of the main features of the SKiPPER-I environment is that it relied on a mostly static execution model for skeletons. More precisely, most of the decisions regarding distribution of computations and scheduling of communications were made at compile-time by a third-party CAD software called SynDEx [11]. This implementation path, while resulting in very efficient distributed executives for "static" – by static we mean that the distribution and scheduling of all communications does not depend on input data and can be predicted at compile-time – did not directly support "dynamic" skeletons, in particular those based upon data or task farming (DF and TF). The intermediate representation of DF and TF was therefore rather awkward in SKiPPER-I, relying on *ad-hoc* auxiliary processes and synchronisation barriers to hide dynamically scheduled communications from the static scheduler [9].

Another point about SKiPPER-I is that the target executable code was MPMD: the final parallel C code took the form of a set of distinct main functions (one per processor), each containing direct calls to the application-specific sequential functions interleaved with communications.

By contrast, execution of skeleton-based applications in SKiPPER-II is carried on by a *single* program (the "kernel" in the sequel) running in SPMD mode on all processors and ensuring a fully *dynamic* distribution and scheduling of processes and communications. The kernel's work is to:

- run the application by interpreting an intermediate description of the application obtained from the CAML program source,
- emulate any skeletons of the previous version of SKiPPER,
- manage resources (processors) for load-balancing when multiple skeletons must run simultaneously.

In SKiPPER-II, the target executable code is therefore made up of the kernel and the application-specific sequential functions. In effect the kernel acts as a small (distributed) operating system that provides all routines the application needs to run on a processor network.

The overall software architecture of the SKiPPER-II programming environment is given on Figure 2: the *skeletal specification* in CAML is analysed to produce the intermediate description which is interpreted at run-time by the kernel; the sequential functions and the kernel code are compiled together to make the target executable code. These points will be detailed in the next sections. Note that figure 2, compared to the corresponding one given for SKiPPER-I (in [20] for example), shows a significant reduction in the number of implementation steps. This of course can be explained by the fact that many decisions that were taken at compile-time in the previous version are now taken dynamically (at run-time) by the kernel.

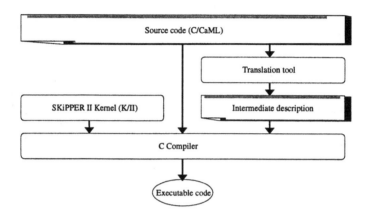

Fig. 2. SKiPPER-II Environment.

3.1 Intermediate description

Clearly, the validity of the "kernel-based" approach presented above depends on the definition of an adequate *intermediate description*. It is the interpretation (at run-time) of this description by the kernel that will trigger the execution of the application-specific sequential functions on the processors, according to the data dependencies encoded by the skeletons.

A key point about SKiPPER-II is that, at this intermediate level of description, all skeletons have been turned into *instances* of a more general one called TF/II. The operational semantics of the TF/II skeleton is similar to the one of DF and TF: a *master* (farmer) process still doles out tasks to a pool of *worker* (slave) processes, but the tasks can now be different (*i.e.* each worker can compute a different function).

The rationale for this "uniformisation" step is three-fold.

– First, it makes skeleton composition easier, because the number of possible combinations now reduces to two (TF/II followed by TF/II or TF/II nested in TF/II).
– Second, it greatly simplifies the structure of the run-time kernel, which only has to know how to run a TF/II skeleton.
– Third, there is only one skeleton code to design and maintain, since all other skeletons will be defined in terms of this generic skeleton.

The above-mentioned transformation is illustrated on Figure 3 with a SCM skeleton. In this figure white boxes represent pure sequential functions and grey boxes "support" processes (parameterised by sequential functions). Note that at the CAML level, the programmer still uses distinct skeletons (SCM, DF, TF,...) when writing the skeletal description of his application. The transformation is done by simply providing alternative definitions of the SCM, DF, TF,... higher-order functions in terms of the TF/II one. Skeleton composition is expressed by normal functional composition. The program appearing in Figure 4, for example, can be written like this in CAML:

```
let nested x = scm 2 s2 f2 m2 x;;
let main x = scm 2 s1 nested m1 x;;
```

The intermediate description itself – as interpreted by the kernel – is a tree of TF/II descriptors, where each node contains informations to identify the next skeleton and to retrieve the C function run by a worker process. Figure 4 shows an example of the corresponding data structure in the case of two nested SCM skeletons. In the current version, the intermediate description is written manually in the form of a C module linked with the kernel/application code before execution. It is intended to be automatically generated from the CAML source program using a modified version of the CAMLFLOW tool [18] already used in SKiPPER-I.

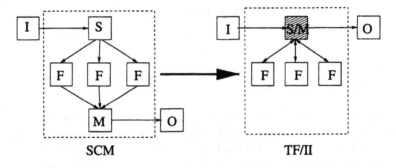

I: input function   S: split function   F: compute function

O: output function   M: merge function

Fig. 3. SCM → TF/II transformation.

3.2 Execution model

Within our fully dynamic execution model, skeletons are viewed as concurrent processes competing for resources on the processor network.

When a skeleton needs to be run, and because any skeleton is now viewed as a TF/II instance, a kernel copy acts as the master process of the TF/II. This copy manages all data transfers between the master and the worker (slave) processes of the TF/II. Slave processes are located on resources allocated *dynamically* by the master. This way kernel copies interact to emulate skeleton behaviour.

This illustrated on Figure 5 with a small program showing two nested SCM skeletons. This figure shows the role of each kernel copy (two per processor in this case) in the execution of the intermediate description resulting from the the transformation of the SCM skeletons into TF/II ones.

Because any kernel copy knows when and where to start a new skeleton without asking information to copies, the scheduling of skeletons can be distributed. Indeed each copy of the kernel has its own copy of the intermediate description of the application. This means that each processor can start the necessary skeleton when it is needed because it knows which skeleton has stopped. A new skeleton is started whenever the previous one (in the intermediate description) ends. The next skeleton is always started on the processor which has run the previous skeleton (because this resource is supposed to be free and closer than the others!).

Because we want to target dedicated and/or embedded platforms, the kernel was designed to work even if the computing nodes are not able to run more than one process at a time (no need for multitasking).

Finally, in the case of a lack of resources the kernel is able to run some of the skeletons in a serial manner, including the whole application, thus providing a straightforward sequential emulation facility for parallel programs.

3.3 Management of Communications

The communication layer is based on a reduced set of the MPI library functions (typically MPI_SSend or MPI_Recv), thus increasing the portability of skeleton-based applications across different parallel platforms. We use only synchronous communication functions whereas asynchronous functions may perform much better in some cases, especially when the platform has a specialised coprocessor for communicating and when communications and processing can overlap. This restriction is a consequence of our original experimental platform which did not support asynchronous communications.

4   Preliminary Experiments

Results presented here are preliminary ones, obtained with a prototype implementation of SKiPPER-II on a cluster of 8 Sun workstations (Sun Ultra 5) interconnected with a 100 Mbits Ethernet network (effective bandwidth is about 8.5 Mbytes/s).

The application used for the benchmark is a "synthetic" one. Even if it is too simple to reflect the complexity of real vision applications, it allows us to easily change its parameters to measure different features of interest. It is composed of two identical SCM skeletons nested in another one (it is very close to the one appearing in Figure 5). The outer SCM skeleton splits the input data (an array of N bytes) into two arrays of size $N/2$. Each inner SCM splits its input array into $n/2$ arrays, where n is the number of available machines (nodes). Each slave computes C/n floating-point operations. The value of N and C may be freely adjusted. This application was also programmed using raw MPI calls, to provide a basis for comparison (in this version, the nested structure of the application has been flattened, *i.e.* we just make a single scatter, followed by a broadcast). For the SKiPPER-II version, we put two kernel copies per node.

Results are given in Figures 6, 7 and 8 for three configurations:

- $C = 100$ MFlops, $N=1$ Mbytes,
- $C = 100$ MFlops, $N=10$ Mbytes,
- $C = 10$ MFlops, $N=10$ Mbytes.

The Figure 6 exhibits a case in which a high compute/communication can in theory lead to almost linear speedups. Here the performances of SKiPPER-II and C/MPI are very close. The overhead of the former – mainly due to kernel – is less is less than 10 %. It can be explained by

- the search for free resources by the kernel (involving a request to a centralised resource manager in the current implementation)
- the need to run inner master processes.

The influence of higher communication costs on the relative performances of the two implementations is evidenced in Figure 7. Here, the fact that SKiPPER-II performs more communications than raw MPI (because of the added communications between the outer and inner masters) results in a significantly higher (up to 50 %) overhead.

This effect has been investigated further in Figure 8 showing a very low compute/communication ratio. Despite the low parallel efficiency of the application – evidenced by the almost non-accelerated MPI version – it is encouraging that the behaviour of SKiPPER-II draws near to the one of the latter when the number of nodes increases.

5 Related Work

The P^3L project [6] [1] [8] [2] has developed a fully-fledged parallel programming language based on the concept of skeletons and associated implementation templates. A distinction is made between task parallel skeletons ("farm" and "pipe"), data parallel skeletons ("map" and "reduce") and control skeletons ("loop"). These skeletons are similar to ours and skeleton nesting is allowed in P^3L. Sequential parts of a P^3L application may be written in many sequential languages (C, Pascal, ...) and skeletons are introduced as special constructs using a C-like syntax. The P^3L compilers generate code for Transputer-based Meiko machines and for PVM running on a cluster of UNIX workstations. Recently Danelutto *et al.* [7] have proposed an integration of the P^3L skeletons within the CaML language, making program specifications looking very similar to ours. Both P^3L and OCamlP^{3}L require either a good OS-level support (UNIX socket) or a generic message passing library (MPI) for their implementation.

Moreover Danelutto *et al.* proposed a new implementation model for skeletons [6] which is based on a distributed Macro Data Flow interpreter. This implementation model is close to ours: the skeleton code (which describes the application) is evaluated at run-time by an interpreter, and this interpreter is distributed. The difference lies in the intermediate representation: a data-flow graph for [6], a tree of TF/II skeletons for SKiPPER-II.

Michaelson *et al.* at Edinburgh also developed a parallel programming system which allows skeleton nesting [16] [13] [12] [14]. They have significant experience in the application of functional programming to vision applications [3] [15]. Skeletons are defined as higher-order functions in ML (as we do), and their latest definition of a vision-specific skeleton basis is very similar to ours (with comparable definitions for the skeletons).

Their implementation, supporting dynamic execution of skeletons, relies on MPI *process groups* to allow concurrent access to computing resources when several skeletons must simultaneously run. This approach requires a message passing layer with routines to manage groups of processes. Our approach does not. Moreover, we never let the message passing layer allocates resources itself: all allocations are made internally by the kernel, allowing some finer decisions to be taken according to the global skeletal structure.

Their work also differs from ours in two other points. First, their goal is an implicitly parallel system within which the decision of expanding a skeleton higher-order function into parallel constructs at the implementation level is taken by the compiler and not in the hand of the programmer. Second, no provision appear to be made for reusing sequential functions written in C (all the program is written in ML).

6 Conclusion and Perspective

The improvements realized in the new version of our SKiPPER parallel programming environment cover two essential aspects in skeleton implementation:

- allowing skeleton composition, and especially the case of skeleton nesting,
- relying on dynamic (runtime) scheduling of skeletons.

The implementation model of skeletons was changed in a way that all skeletons can now be described using the same execution model. This was achieved by reformulating all skeletons as instances of a very general purpose one: the TF/II skeleton. This point offers possibilities in optimising the application since transformation rules could be applied to the TF/II tree.

Preliminary experiments show that skeleton nesting after conversion of all skeletons in TF/II is easy to do and that, at least in the tested operational conditions, the cost penalty associated with the new implementation and execution models is not prohibitive (compared to hand-written MPI code).

Work remains to be done to further assess the performances of SKiPPER-II on larger scale platforms. To do so, investigations are planned on a Cray T3E and large workstation clusters [1].

---

[1] These investigations are planned under the TRACS European Commission programme, at Edinburgh Parallel Computing Center in February and March 2001.

References

[1] B. Bacci, B. Cantalupo, M. Danelutto, S. Orlando, D. Pasetto, S. Pelagatti, and M. Vanneschi. An environment for structured parallel programming. In L. Grandinetti, M. Kowalick, and M. Vaitersic, editors, *Advances in High Performance Computing*, pages 219–234. Kluwier, Dordrecht, The Netherlands, 1997.

[2] B. Bacci, M. Danelutto, S. Orlando, S. Pelagatti, and M. Vanneschi. P^{3}L: A structured high level programming language and its structured support. *Concurrency: Practice and Experience*, 7(3):225–255, May 1995.

[3] T.A. Bratvold. *Skeleton-based Parallelisation of Functional Programs*. PhD thesis, Heriot-Watt University, Department of Computing and Electrical Engineering, November 1994.

[4] M. Cole. *Algorithmic skeletons: structured management of parallel computations*. Pitman/MIT Press, 1989.

[5] M. Cole. *Research Directions in Parallel Functional Programming*, chapter Algorithmic Skeletons, pp 289–303. K. Hammond and G. Michaelson Eds, Springer UK, November 1999.

[6] M. Danelutto. Dynamic run time support for skeletons. *Proceedings of the ParCo99 Conference, Delft, the Netherlands*, August 1999.

[7] M. Danelutto, R. DiCosmo, X. Leroy, and S. Pelagatti. Parallel functional programming with skeletons: the ocamlp3l experiment. In *Proceedings ACM workshop on ML and its applications, Cornell university*, 1998.

[8] M. Danelutto, F. Pasqualetti, and S. Pelagatti. Skeletons for data parallelism in p3l. In C. Lengauer, M. Griebl, and S. Gorlatch, editors, *Proc. of EURO-PAR '97, Passau, Germany*, volume 1300 of *LNCS*, pages 619–628. Springer, August 1997.

[9] D. Ginhac. *Prototypage rapide d'applications parallèles de vision artificielle par squelettes fonctionnels*. PhD thesis, Université Blaise-Pascal, Clermont-Ferrand, France, January 1999.

[10] D. Ginhac, J. Sérot, and J.-P. Dérutin. Fast prototyping of image processing applications using functional skeletons on mimd-dm architecture. In *IAPR Workshop on Machine Vision Applications*, pages 468–471, November 1998.

[11] T. Grandpierre, C. Lavarenne, and Y. Sorel. Optimized rapid prototyping for real time embedded heterogeneous multiprocessors. *CODES'99 7th International Workshop on Hardware/Software Co-Design, Rome*, May 1999.

[12] M. Hamdan. *A Combinational Framework for Parallel Programming using Algorithmic Skeletons*. PhD thesis, Heriot-Watt University, Department of Computing and Electrical Engineering, January 2000.

[13] M. Hamdan, G. Michaelson, and P. King. A scheme for nesting algorithmic skeletons. *IFL'98, Clack, T. Davie and K. Hammond (eds): Proceedings of 10th International Workshop on Implementation of Functional Languages, University College London*, pages 195–212, September 1998.

[14] G. Michaelson, N. Scaife, P. Bristow, and P. King. Nested algorithmic skeletons from higher order functions. *Parallel Algorithms and Applications special issue on High Level Models and Languages for Parallel Processing*, 2000.

[15] G. Michaelson and N.R. Scaife. Prototyping a parallel vision system in standard ml. *Journal of Functional Programming*, 5(3):345–382, 1995.

[16] N. Scaife. *A Dual Source Parallel Architecture for Computer Vision*. PhD thesis, Heriot-Watt University, Department of Computing and Electrical Engineering, May 2000.

[17] J. Sérot. Embodying parallel functional skeletons: an experimental implementation on top of mpi. In C. Lengauer, M. Griebl, and S. Gorlatch, editors, *3rd Intl Euro-Par Conference on Parallel Processing*, pages 629–633. Springer, 26-29 August 1999.

[18] J. Sérot. Camlflow: a caml to data-flow translator. In *Proceedings of the 2nd Scottish Functional Programming Workshop, St-Andrews*, 27-29 July 2000.

[19] J. Sérot, D. Ginhac, R. Chapuis, and J.-P. Dérutin. Fast prototyping of parallel vision applications using functional skeletons. *To appear in International Journal of Machine Vision and Application*, 2001.

[20] J. Sérot, D. Ginhac, and J.-P. Dérutin. Skipper: a skeleton-based parallel programming environment for real-time image processing applications. In V. Malyshkin, editor, *5th International Conference on Parallel Computing Technologies (PaCT-99)*, volume 1662 of *LNCS*, pages 296–305. Springer, 6–10 September 1999.

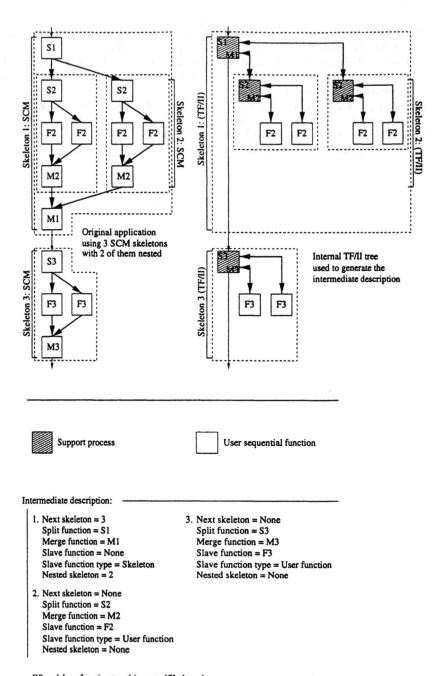

Original application
using 3 SCM skeletons
with 2 of them nested

Internal TF/II tree
used to generate the
intermediate description

▨ Support process

☐ User sequential function

Intermediate description:

1. Next skeleton = 3
   Split function = S1
   Merge function = M1
   Slave function = None
   Slave function type = Skeleton
   Nested skeleton = 2

2. Next skeleton = None
   Split function = S2
   Merge function = M2
   Slave function = F2
   Slave function type = User function
   Nested skeleton = None

3. Next skeleton = None
   Split function = S3
   Merge function = M3
   Slave function = F3
   Slave function type = User function
   Nested skeleton = None

When 'slave function type' is set to 'Skeleton'
then 'Nested skeleton' field is used to know
which skeleton must be used as a slave, that is
to say which skeleton must be nested in.

Fig. 4. Intermediate description data structure example.

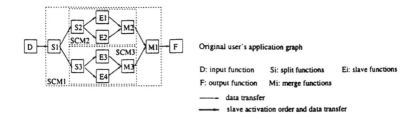

Original user's application graph

D: input function   Si: split functions   Ei: slave functions

F: output function   Mi: merge functions

——   data transfer

——▶   slave activation order and data transfer

Execution of the application on 4 processors with 8 kernel copies

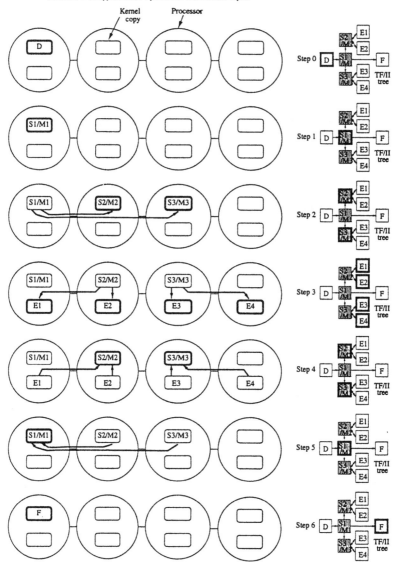

Fig. 5. Example of the execution of two SCM nested in one SCM.

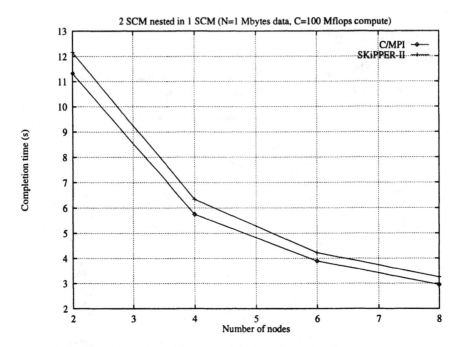

Fig. 6. SKiPPER-II and C/MPI implementations comparison for C=100 MFlops/N=1 Mbytes.

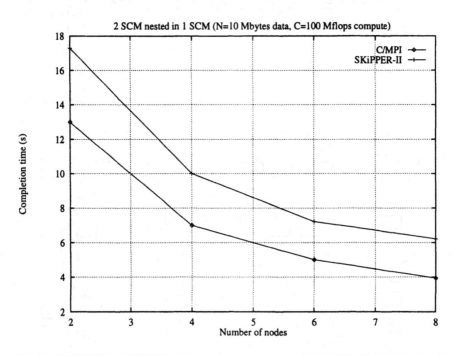

Fig. 7. SKiPPER-II and C/MPI implementations comparison for C=100 MFlops/N=10 Mbytes.

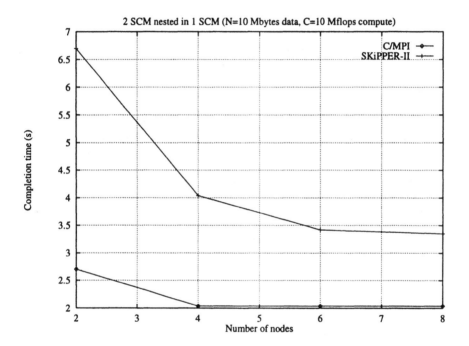

Fig. 8. SKiPPER-II and C/MPI implementations comparison for C=10 MFlops/N=10 Mbytes.

Supporting Soft Real-Time Tasks and QoS on the Java Platform

James C. Pang[1], Gholamali C. Shoja[2], and Eric G. Manning[2]

[1] Current affiliation: Redback Networks. This author was supported in part by
Natural Sciences and Engineering Research Council (NSERC) of Canada, and
Sony Corporation.
jcpang@Redback.com

[2] Department of Computer Science, University of Victoria,
Victoria, BC, V8W 3P6, Canada
{gshoja,emanning}@csr.UVic.ca

Abstract. The Java platform has many characteristics which make it very desirable for integrated continuous media processing. Unfortunately, it lacks the necessary CPU resource management facility to support Quality of Service guarantees for soft real-time multimedia tasks. In this paper, we present our new Java Virtual Machine, Q-JVM, which brings CPU resource management to the Java platform. Q-JVM is based on Sun's reference implementation. It incorporates an enhanced version of the MTR-LS algorithm in its thread scheduler. Combined with an optional admission control mechanism, this algorithm is able to support QoS parameters such as fairness, bandwidth partitioning and delay bound guarantees, as well as the cumulative service guarantee. Preliminary experimental results show that Q-JVM is backward compatible with the standard version from Sun, has low scheduling overhead, and is able to provide QoS guarantees as specified.

1 Introduction

Integrated continuous media processing presents unique challenges to the underlying computational environment: it imposes real-time requirements on the host operating system and its subsystems, as continuous media data must be presented continuously in time at a predetermined rate in order to convey their meaning. However, software that process continuous media data is often classified as being *soft real-time*, as missing a particular deadline is not fatal as long as it is not missed by too much and most other deadlines are not missed.

The Java platform [1] has many desirable characteristics for integrated multimedia processing. Java is a simple and small language. It is object-oriented and supports many language features such as interfaces and automatic memory management, which make it a robust environment for software development. It also supports multithreading at the language level with built-in synchronization primitives, thus allowing a high degree of interactivity with the end user. Moreover, Java has a rich collection of application programming interfaces which support media manipulation and continuous media processing. Most importantly, Java was designed for embedded applications, and is ideal for media-capable integrated devices of the future.

Unfortunately, Java does not have the facility to support soft real-time tasks. Real-time programming is a matter of managing resources, most notably the CPU resource. However, Java does not provide any mechanism which can be used to monitor, manage, or police the usage of the CPU resource.

In this paper, we present a new Java Virtual Machine with QoS features, the Q-JVM, based on Sun's JVM. Its purpose is to support integrated continuous media processing on mobile or embedded devices, such as PDAs and TV set-top boxes, where soft real-time guarantees must be provided with limited system resources.

Our new JVM employs an enhanced version of the Move-To-Rear List Scheduling algorithm [2] in its thread scheduler. The service fraction-based scheduling algorithm is enhanced to handle not only user threads, but also system threads which must express their urgency using priorities.

Preliminary test results have shown that Q-JVM has low scheduling overhead, and is able to provide QoS guarantees as specified. Moreover, it is binary compatible with the standard JVM distributed by Sun.

The rest of this paper is organized as follows. Section 2 discusses related research in resource and Quality of Service management. Section 3 describes our implementation of Q-JVM which supports CPU resource management and some of our experiments with this platform. Finally, Section 4 briefly summarizes this paper.

2   Previous Work

There has been a lot of research in CPU resource management for soft real-time applications. Some researchers have studied existing systems and algorithms that claim to support real-time multimedia applications [7]. At the same time others like [5] have borrowed ideas from link scheduling, or have proposed new algorithms [2] for managing the CPU resource.

2.1   Static Priority based Scheduling

The most common CPU resource management schemes employ static priority-based scheduling. In such a scheme, all execution entities are assigned fixed priorities. The scheduler rations the CPU among competing scheduling entities according to their priorities. However, an extensive quantitative analysis of such a scheduler, as implemented in UNIX System V Release 4, demonstrated that it is largely ineffective in dealing with soft real-time tasks [7]. It could even produce system lockup.

Similarly, hard real-time scheduling algorithms, such as Earliest Deadline First and the Rate Monotonic Algorithm, are also not suitable for integrated continuous media processing [7]. This class of algorithms either fails to achieve the desired efficiency for integrated computing environments, or requires prior analysis of computational requirements of the particular application mix. The latter is difficult, if not impossible, for dynamic systems.

2.2 Resource Management Based on Fair Queuing

Network bandwidth resource management has long been a hot research topic. A large body of work exists in the scheduling of network flows to network links. Many researchers have noticed the parallel between CPU scheduling and network link scheduling. Thus, it is not surprising that many link scheduling algorithms have been adopted for CPU scheduling. Among these, the Start-time Fair Queuing (SFQ) algorithm [5] is a notable example.

SFQ improves upon early fair queuing algorithms like Weighted Fair Queuing [3] and Self Clocked Fair Queuing [4] by removing their requirement for prior knowledge of the computational needs of competing tasks; it is also much more efficient than algorithms like Fair Queuing based on Start time [5]. Moreover, it handles fluctuation in available bandwidth due to sporadic interrupt processing better than other fair queuing algorithms [5]. Unfortunately, its delay bound increases linearly with the number of threads in the system [8], thus making it undesirable for complex and dynamic systems.

2.3 The MTR-LS algorithm

The Move-To-Rear List Scheduling algorithm (MTR-LS) is a resource scheduling algorithm which was developed at the Bell Laboratories to provide predictable service in a general purpose system with multiple resources including CPU, disk, and a network [2]. Besides the usual Quality of Service parameters such as fairness, bandwidth partitioning and delay bound, it also supports a new criterion called *cumulative service guarantee*: MTR-LS guarantees that the real service obtained by a process, given its specified service rate, on a shared server does not fall behind the ideal service it would have accumulated on a dedicated server at the same service rate, by more than a constant amount.

Scheduling using MTR-LS is based on *service fractions*. A service fraction is a fraction assigned to a scheduling entity that represents the service rate of a virtual server in terms of the real server. A system constant, named the *virtual time quantum* T, is used to specify the total target time for servicing each and every active scheduling entity in the system exactly once.

Each scheduling entity is also assigned a time stamp and a quantum *left* when it requests service. The quantum size is calculated as the product of its service fraction and T. All active scheduling entities are kept in the *service list*, and are sorted by their time stamps. Entities with earlier time stamps appear closer to the front of the list. The MTR-LS algorithm always schedules the first runnable entity on the service list.

A scheduled entity is preempted when its quantum expires or when some other entity whose position on the service list is ahead of it becomes runnable. After the preemption, the time it has been serviced on the server is subtracted from its quantum *left*, to yield an updated value of *left*. If the result is zero, then it is assigned a new time stamp and its quantum is re-initialized. Its position on the *service list* is adjusted according to its new time stamp; i.e., it is moved to the rear of the list.

The MTR-LS algorithm provides bandwidth partitioning and fairness guarantees for all competing entities with respect to their service fraction allocations. With admission control, it is also able to provide delay bounds and cumulative service guarantees [2]. Moreover, it is very efficient: even with a straightforward implementation, the computational complexity of the algorithm is $O(ln(n))$ where n is the number of entries in the service list [2]. These properties persuaded us to build on the MTR-LS algorithm to provide Quality of Service guarantees for Java threads.

3 Q-JVM

Our enhanced version of JVM is based on Sun's reference implementation of the Java virtual machine. The JVM source code obtained from Sun supports both the Windows and Solaris platforms; however, we chose to develop our Q-JVM on Solaris.

Java threads may be mapped on to native operating system scheduling entities using *One*-to-*One*, *Many*-to-*One* or *Many*-to-*Many* models [6]. With a 1-to-1 mapping, each Java thread is supported by its own scheduling entity known to the operating system. Scheduling is handled by the OS kernel; all threads have equal access to the kernel at the same time. Thus, this model is able to exploit any hardware parallelism that may be present.

With the m-to-1 model, all Java threads are mapped onto the same scheduling entity supported by the OS, and scheduling of Java threads is handled by a user-level threads library. Only one scheduling entity is known to the operating system, and only one thread can access the kernel at any given time. This model does not exploit hardware parallelism; however, it has the advantage that the OS kernel is not required to support multithreading. Moreover, it is also very efficient, as all scheduling decisions and context switches can be handled in user space, without kernel intervention. This is a considerable advantage in uni-processor environments where additional expensive context switches to and from the kernel does not yield any benefit in terms of increased parallelism. It is thus ideal for mobile and embedded devices that do not have multiple processors, and where CPU bandwidth is at a premium.

The m-to-n mapping model is the most elaborate. It uses a user-level threads library in conjunction with an OS kernel that supports multi-threading: Java threads are mapped onto a pool of scheduling entities known to the kernel. The threads library manages the pool of scheduling entities and the mapping between Java threads and kernel scheduling entities, while the kernel schedules only the entities known to it.

On Solaris, one has the option of using either the *Many*-to-*Many* model with the Solaris native thread library, or the *Many*-to-*One* model with the Green Thread library. Since it is not common to have true hardware parallelism on our target platform, we decided to base our changes on Green Thread using the m-to-1 model.

Our approach is to build the resource management facility into the lowest level of the JVM, in this case the Green Thread library, so that resource consumption by all threads, including the threads spawned by the JVM and its native libraries, can be managed effectively.

3.1 Extension to Green Thread

Green Thread is a traditional priority-based threads package. It relies on three system threads for its operation, and it uses a stateless scheduler function which runs on the preempted thread's stack. It is also tightly integrated with the Java virtual machine.

Scheduling in Green Thread is based on priority. Priorities are represented by integer values, where larger integers represent higher priority. Although the basic architecture does not limit the range of priorities, user threads use only ten values: integers from 10 to 1. Java threads use only these priority values as well.

There are three system threads in Green Thread that use priorities outside of the range for user threads (Figure 1). These system threads are the *ClockHandler* thread (priority 12), the *TimeSlicer* thread (priority 11), and the *Idler* thread (priority 0).

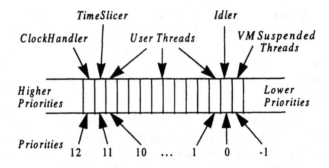

Figure 1. Priorities of Green Threads

Our purpose is to support soft real-time scheduling of Green threads (and in turn, Java threads) through the addition of a resource management algorithm to the Green Thread library. In our final implementation, Green Thread's system threads and the monitor infrastructure were largely unchanged. However, the thread private data structure, the queues and the scheduler function were extended to accommodate the new scheduling policy. The preemption and context switching mechanisms were also modified to track CPU resource consumption by individual threads.

The first change is to extend the thread data structure to include fields for a time stamp, a service fraction specification, and the time left in a thread's current quantum, i.e., the *left* value. The service fraction is specified by the user, and may be changed at any time. It is used to calculate a thread's quantum, in conjunction with the virtual time quantum. The time stamp is used to determine the position of a thread in the *service list*: threads having earlier time stamps appear at nearer the head of the list than threads with later ones. When a thread finishes a quantum, it is assigned a new (later) time stamp and thus moved to the rear of the list. Green Thread's runnable queue is also modified to enable scheduling according to time stamp.

Green Thread's context switching code is also modified to take a reading of the system clock every time a thread is scheduled, and another one when the thread is preempted. The elapsed time is subtracted from the *left* value of this thread.

When invoked, a new Green Thread scheduler fetches the thread with the earliest time stamp from the runnable queue and checks its *left* value. If this value is less than or equal to zero, it moves this thread to the rear of the list by assigning it a new time stamp and reinserting it into the runnable queue. The *left* of this thread is re-initiated to be $\alpha \cdot T + left$, where α is the service fraction of this thread, T is the virtual time quantum, and *left* is this thread's last *left* value. The scheduler function repeats this operation until it finds a thread with a positive *left* value. It then invokes the context switching code to record the start time of this quantum and transfer the control of CPU to the scheduled thread.

3.2   Extension to the MTR-LS Algorithm

The MTR-LS algorithm is used in Q-JVM to schedule not only user threads, but also system threads that must express their urgency using priorities. For example, the thread scheduler must recognize that the *ClockHandler* thread must be scheduled as soon as it is runnable and the *idler* thread should only be scheduled when there are no other runnable threads. Unfortunately, MTR-LS is based on service fractions and CPU resource consumption. It does not have an inherent notion of urgency, which may be expressed with priorities.

Our solution is to extend the MTR-LS algorithm to handle the system threads as a special case. We took advantage of the fact that MTR-LS schedules threads according to their positions on the *service list L*, and that the time stamps which determine the positions of threads on L can serve as effective priorities.

Under the MTR-LS algorithm, a thread will not be scheduled if there are other threads ahead of it on the service list. Hence, if high priority system threads are placed at the beginning of the list ahead of all user threads, then as soon as they become runnable they will be scheduled. Similarly, if the low priority system threads are placed at the rear of the list after all user threads, then they will not be scheduled until there are no user threads that are runnable.

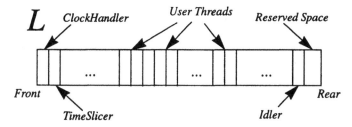

Figure 2. Positions of the System Threads and User Threads on the Service List L.

A map of positions of the system threads and user threads on the service list L is shown in Figure 2. The *ClockHandler* thread and the *TimeSlicer* thread are assigned the two earliest (largest) time stamps. This puts them at the beginning of the service list. At the same time, the *idler* thread is assigned an artificially late (small) time stamp which puts it near the end of the service list[1]. Moreover, all system threads are tagged so that when context is switched away from them, their *left* values are not updated. As a result, their positions on *L* are stationary.

This approach takes full advantage of the natural ordering of threads on the *service list* and the parallel between time stamps and global priorities. It provides a simple and straightforward solution to the problem of using the MTR-LS algorithm in a root scheduler which must allow system threads to express their urgency.

3.3 High Level API

The enhanced capabilities of Q-JVM are made available to the application layer via a high level API consisting of two Java classes: the QThread class and the QThread-Group class. These two classes supersede the java.lang.Thread class and the java.lang.ThreadGroup class, respectively.

The QThread class provides CPU resource management capabilities to Java threads. It supports all normal threads operations such as thread creation, termination and communication. At the same time, it supports specification of resource requirements in terms of service fraction reservations. The QThreadGroup class provides support for CPU bandwidth partitioning for groups of threads.

The java.lang.Thread class and the java.lang.ThreadGroup class were also re-implemented to provide compatibility. These classes adapt the classic Thread API to Q-JVM in order to support unmodified legacy Java programs.

3.4 Experiments and Results

The preliminary performance evaluation was done on a Sun SPARCserver 20 with a 60MHz Ultra-SPARC CPU and 64 MB of main memory running Solaris 2.4. The experiments were conducted in multi-user mode with the standard complement of daemons like *lpd*, *sendmail*, *NFS*, and a very lightly loaded *HTTP* server. Moreover, all experiments were conducted when there was no interactive user activities.

Most of the experiments were carried out using the *RaceTest* test suite. This test suite is a multithreaded Java program that simulates a CPU intensive application. It is modeled after the well known *Dhrystone* benchmark. When the application starts, it spawns a number of threads, called *runners*, each of which executes an arithmetic calculation repeatedly in a loop. The number of loops completed in a given time by one or more *runners* is used as the performance metric.

Two versions of the test suite were constructed. The first one runs on the enhanced JVM and allows an operator to specify the number of *runners* to start and the service fraction for each *runner*. The other version runs on the standard JVM. Instead of service fractions, it allows an operator to specify priorities for the *runners*. Otherwise, the two versions are identical. A standard Java virtual machine was built from the un-modified JVM source from Sun to run the standard version of *RaceTest*.

---

1. The last few positions on *L* are reserved for implementing a JVM system function which suspends all user threads before the garbage collector is invoked. The original implementation sets the priorities of all user threads to -1. Our implementation moves the user threads to a position on *L* that is behind the *idler* thread.

A major concern in using a complex resource management scheme such as the one built into our enhanced Java virtual machine is that the scheduling overhead may be high. To evaluate this overhead, we compared the aggregate average throughput achieved by the Race Test application on the enhanced platform versus the standard JVM. The results are presented in Table 1 below.

Table 1: Effect of Scheduling Overhead on Thread Throughput

	1 *Runner*	4 *Runners*	10 *Runners*
Standard JVM	602,797	602,084	601,040
Q-JVM Configuration 1	601,399	599,860	599,714
Q-JVM Configuration 2	601,582	600,939	599,882

All reported figures in the above table are Aggregate Average Throughput in loops completed per second. This figure is arrived at as follows. One thousand throughput samples are taken for each runner. If there is only one thread, the average is reported. When there is more than one runner, the sum of their averages is reported.

On the standard JVM, all threads (runners) are started with priority 5. On the enhanced JVM, all threads are assigned 1.5% of total CPU bandwidth in configuration 1. In configuration 2, all threads are assigned equal service fractions totaling 80%. For example, when there are 10 threads, each is assigned a service fraction of 8%.

From Table 1 we can observe that the throughput differences among all figures are very small: throughput of the application running on Q-JVM is only 0.19% and 0.36% lower than the same application running on the standard JVM. As the application is CPU intensive, and does not involve any I/O or kernel service call, this result indicates that the additional scheduling overhead of the new platform is very small compared to the standard Java virtual machine.

With the same application and similar test procedures, we also demonstrated that Q-JVM is able to provide predictable resource allocation and resource partitioning with service fraction specifications. Table 2 shows result from one test run with 2 runners. One is assigned service fractions of 70% and the other 20%; their respective throughputs are 73% and 26% of the total throughput.

Table 2: Resource Allocation and Partitioning.

	Service Fraction	Throughput (% of total)
Runner 1	70%	442,728 (74%)
Runner 2	20%	158,069 (26%)

In addition to the *RaceTest* application, a number of standard test suites and application such as the *CaffeineMark* suite, the *Java Media Framework*, and the *HotJava* browser were successfully executed on the Q-JVM without any modifications. The results indicated that the new platform is binary compatible with the standard JVM distributed by Sun.

4 Summary

In this paper, we presented our work on supporting soft real-time tasks on the Java platform. We developed a new JVM that is able to support resource allocation and regulation of consumption of the CPU resource.

We extended a service fraction-based resource management algorithm, the Move-to-Rear List-Scheduling algorithm, to handle system threads that must express their urgency, normally expressed using priorities. We then incorporated this algorithm into a new JVM based on the source code of the JVM licensed from Sun.

The result of our work is a new Java platform that is able to support soft real-time tasks. It provides mechanisms for resource allocation and management, as well as guarantees for a number of quality of service parameters like fairness, bandwidth partitioning and cumulative service.

Preliminary test results indicate that our scheme for resource accounting and management is viable and the new Q-JVM is indeed able to provide these QoS guarantees as specified. Yet, its scheduling overhead is similar to that of the standard version. Moreover, our JVM is binary compatible with the standard JVM distributed by Sun.

References

1. K. Arnold and J. Gosling. The Java Programming Language, Second Edition. Addision-Wesley, Reading, Massachusetts. 1998.
2. J. Bruno, E. Gabber, B. Ozden, and A. Silberschatz. Move-To-Rear List Scheduling: a new scheduling algorithm for providing QoS guarantees. In *Proceedings of The Fifth ACM International Multimedia Conference*, pp. 63-73, November 9-13, 1997.
3. A. Demers, S. Keshav, and S. Shenker. Analysis and Simulation of a Fair Queueing Algorithm. In *Proceedings of ACM SIGCOMM*, pp. 1-12, September 1989.
4. S. J. Golestani. A Self-Clocked Fair Queueing Scheme for Broadband Applications. In *Proceedings of the 13th Annual Joint Conference of the IEEE Computer and Communications Societies on Networking for Global Communication*. 2:636-646, IEEE Computer Society Press, June 1994.
5. P. Goyal, X. Guo, and H.M. Vin. A Hierarchical CPU Scheduler for Multimedia Operating Systems. In *Proceedings of the Second USENIX Symposium on Operating System Design and Implementation*, pp. 107-121, October 1996.
6. JavaSoft. Multithreaded Implementation and Comparisons, A White Paper. *Available at http://solaris.javasoft.com/developer/news/whitepapers/mtwp.html*. Part No.: 96168-001. JavaSoft. April 1996.
7. J. Nieh et al., "SVR4 UNIX Scheduler Unacceptable for Multimedia Applications", *Lecture Notes in Computer Science*, Vol. 846, D. Shepherd et al. (eds.), Springer Verlag, Heidelberg, Germany, 1994, pp. 41-53.
8. I. Stoica et. al., A Proportional Share Resource Allocation Algorithm for Real-Time, Time-Shared Systems. In *Proceedings of the IEEE Real Time Systems Symposium*, Dec. 1996.

Evaluating the XMT Parallel Programming Model

Dorit Naishlos[1] *, Joseph Nuzman[2][3] *, Chau-Wen Tseng[1][3], Uzi Vishkin[2][3][4] *

[1] Dept of Computer Science, University of Maryland, College Park, MD 20742
[2] Dept of Electrical and Computer Engineering, University of Maryland, College Park, MD 20742
[3] University of Maryland Institute of Advanced Computer Studies, College Park, MD 20742
[4] Dept of Computer Science, Technion – Israel Institute of Technology, Haifa 32000, Israel
{dorit, jnuzman, tseng, vishkin}@cs.umd.edu

Abstract. Explicit-multithreading (XMT) is a parallel programming model designed for exploiting on-chip parallelism. Its features include a simple thread execution model and an efficient prefix-sum instruction for synchronizing shared data accesses. By taking advantage of low-overhead parallel threads and high on-chip memory bandwidth, the XMT model tries to reduce the burden on programmers by obviating the need for explicit task assignment and thread coarsening. This paper presents features of the XMT programming model, and evaluates their utility through experiments on a prototype XMT compiler and architecture simulator. We find the lack of explicit task assignment has slight effects on performance for the XMT architecture. Despite low thread overhead, thread coarsening is still necessary to some extent, but can usually be automatically applied by the XMT compiler. The prefix-sum instruction provides more scalable synchronization than traditional locks, and the simple run-until-completion thread execution model (no busy-waits) does not impair performance. Finally, the combination of features in XMT can encourage simpler parallel algorithms that may be more efficient than more traditional complex approaches.

1 Introduction

When discussing parallel programming models, the parallel computing community usually considers two models: message-passing and shared-memory. Both models usually require domain partitioning and load balancing. For dynamic, adaptive applications this effort can amount to 25% of the entire code and become a significant source of overhead [9], [12]. Message-passing in addition requires distributing data structures across processors and explicitly handling inter-processor communication. Performance also decreases for fine-grained parallelism under both models, as the effects of synchronization and communication overhead become a bigger factor.

---

* Supported by NSF grant 9820955.

Many of these issues, however, are of lesser importance for exploiting on-chip parallelism, where parallelism overhead is low and memory bandwidth is high. This observation motivated the development of the Explicit Multi-threading (XMT) programming model. XMT is intended to provide a parallel programming model which is simpler to use, yet efficiently exploits on-chip parallelism

Previous papers on XMT have discussed in detail its fine-grained SPMD multi-threaded programming model, architectural support for concurrently executing multiple contexts on-chip, and preliminary evaluation of several parallel algorithms using hand-coded assembly programs [14] [6]. A more recent paper describes the prototype XMT programming environment, including the XMT compiler and simulator [11]. In this paper, we describe features of the XMT programming model that were designed for exploiting on-chip parallelism, and evaluate their impact on both programmability and performance using the XMT programming environment.

The main contributions of this paper are as follows:

- We discuss and evaluate features of XMT designed to exploit on-chip parallelism.
- We examine their effect on programmability for several interesting application kernels.
- We experimentally evaluate the impact of XMT features on performance using the XMT compiler and simulator.

We begin by reviewing the XMT multi-threaded programming model. We then briefly discuss the XMT architecture and environment, including a compiler and behavioral simulator. We examine the impact of each feature of XMT on programmability and performance. Finally, we present a comparison with related work and conclude.

2 XMT Programming Model

The basic premise behind XMT is that instead of forcing the hardware to find instruction-level parallelism at run-time, the instruction set architecture should provide programmers (or the compiler) with the ability to explicitly specify parallelism when it is available.

The XMT architecture is specifically designed to exploit parallelism in an on-chip environment, in a manner that directly affects the way programs are written in XMT. The XMT architecture attempts to provide more uniform memory access latencies, taking advantage of faster on-chip communication times. In addition, a specialized hardware primitive (prefix-sum), exploits the high on-chip communication bandwidth to provide low overhead thread creation. These low overheads allow to efficiently support fine-grained parallelism. Fine granularity is in turn used to hide memory latencies which, in addition to the more uniform memory accesses, supports a programming model where locality is less of an issue. The XMT hardware also supports dynamic load balancing, relieving the programmers of the task of assigning work to processors. The programming model is simplified further by letting threads always run to completion without synchronization (no busy-waits), and synchronizing accesses to shared data with a prefix-sum instruction. All these features result in a flexible programming style, that encourages the development of new algorithms, and as such, is expected to target a wider range of applications.

The programming model underlying the XMT framework is an arbitrary CRCW (concurrent read concurrent write) SPMD (single program multiple data) programming model. In the XMT programming model, an arbitrary number of virtual threads, initiated by a spawn and terminated by a join, share the same code. At run-time, different threads may have different lengths, based on control flow decisions made at run time. The arbitrary CRCW aspect dictates that concurrent writes to the same memory location result in an arbitrary one committing. No assumption can be made beforehand about which will succeed. This permits each thread to progress at its own speed from its initiating spawn to its terminating join, without ever having to wait for other threads; that is, no thread busy-waits for another thread. An advantage of using this SPMD model is that it is an extension of the classical PRAM model, for which a vast body of parallel algorithms is available in the literature.

The user-level XMT language is an extension of standard C. The following example XMT program copies all non-zero values of array A to B in an arbitrary order:

```
m = 0;
spawn(n,0);
    {
            int TID;
            if (A[TID] != 0) {
                    int k = ps(&m,1);
                    B[k] = A[TID];
            }
    }
join();
```

The programming model has a number of key features:
- Explicit spawn-join parallel regions
- Shared accesses synchronized with prefix-sum instruction
- Threads run to completion (do not busy-wait)
- Dynamic *forking* of additional virtual threads

A parallel region is delineated by *spawn* and *join* statements. Every thread executing the parallel code is assigned a unique thread ID, designated TID. Shared accesses are synchronized with a prefix-sum instruction (*ps*), similar to an atomic fetch-and-increment. It can be combined by the hardware to form a multi-operand prefix-sum operation. XMT does not allow for nested initiation of a spawn within a parallel spawn region [14], but a thread can perform a fork operation to introduce a new virtual thread as work is discovered [15].

3 XMT Architecture

The XMT programming model allows programmers to specify an arbitrary degree of parallelism in their code. Clearly, real hardware has finite execution resources so all threads can't run simultaneously. In an XMT machine, a thread control unit (TCU) executes an individual virtual thread. Upon termination, the TCU performs a prefix-sum operation in order to receive a new thread ID. The TCU will then emulate the thread with that ID. All TCUs repeat the process until all the virtual threads have been completed. This functionality is enabled by support at the instruction set level. With our architecture, all TCUs independently execute a serial program. Each accepts the standard MIPS instructions, and possesses a standard set of MIPS registers locally. The expanded ISA includes a set of specialized global registers, called prefix-sum registers (PR), and a few additional instructions.

New instructions were added for thread management. A spawn instruction interrupts all TCUs and broadcasts a new PC at which all TCUs will start. The *pinc* instruction operates on the PR registers and performs a parallel prefix-sum with value 1. A specialized global prefix-sum unit can handle multiple pincs to the same PR register in parallel. Simultaneous pincs from different TCUs are grouped and the prefix-sum is computed and broadcast back to the TCUs. This process is pipelined, and completes within a constant number of cycles. *pread* performs a parallel read (prefix-sum with value 0) of a PR register, and *pset* is used (serially) to initialize a PR register.

The *psm* instruction allows for communication and synchronization between threads. It performs a prefix-sum operation with an arbitrary increment to any location in memory. It is an atomic operation, but due to hardware limitations, is not performed in parallel (i.e., concurrent psm's will be queued). This is equivalent to a fetch-and-increment. A ps command at the XMT-C level is translated to a psm instruction.

Additional instructions exist to support the nested forking mechanism. Forks from many TCUs can be performed in parallel batches.

4 XMT Environment

The XMT environment consists of a prototype XMT compiler and behavioral simulator. The XMT compiler consists of two passes. The front end is a translator based on the *SUIF* compiler system [17] that converts XMT constructs into regular C code with assembly templates. It also detects all parallel regions delineated by spawn-join statements and transforms them into parallel function calls. The back end is based on GNU's *gcc* and builds an executable for the C code output by the front end [11].

The XMT behavioral simulator is comparable to SimpleScalar [2]. The fundamental units of execution for the simulated machine are the multiple thread control units (TCUs), each of which contains a separate execution context. In hardware, an individual TCU basically consists of the fetch and decode stages of a simple pipelined processor. To increase resource utilization and to hide latencies, sets of TCUs are grouped together to form a cluster. The TCUs in a cluster share a common pool of functional units, as well as memory access and prefix-sum resources. The clusters can be replicated repeatedly on a given chip [3].

For our experiments, we specify 8 TCUs in each cluster. Each cluster contains 4 integer ALUs, 2 integer multiply/divide units, 2 floating point ALUs, 2 floating point multiply/divide units, and 2 branch units. All functional unit latencies are set to the

SimpleScalar sim-outorder defaults: 1 cycle for integer ALU ops, 3 cycles for integer multiply, 20 cycles for integer divide, 2 cycles for floating point ALU ops, 4 cycles for floating point multiply, 12 cycles for floating point divide, and 24 cycles for square root. Each cluster has a L1 cache of 8 KB, and a shared, banked L2 cache of 1 MB. The number of banks is chosen to be twice the number of clusters. The L2 cache latency is 6 cycles and memory latency 25 cycles. A penalty of 4 cycles is charged each way for inter-cluster communication.

5 XMT Programming and Performance

Traditional shared memory programming consists of assigning chunks of work to processes, usually as coarse-grained as possible, while locks and barriers are used for synchronization. The following are the main programming concepts that distinguish XMT from traditional parallel programming:
1. No task assignment.
2. Fine-grained parallelism.
3. No busy-wait.
In this section we examine each of the above features, and how they affect the way programs are written in XMT. Furthermore, we study the effects of these features on performance.

5.1 No Task Assignment

XMT relieves the programmer from the task of assigning work to processors. The programmer can think in terms of virtual threads, without worrying about low-level considerations such as the number of processing units and load balance between them. Instead of directly spawning a thread for each block of work, traditional parallel programming puts a lot of effort into the task of grouping blocks of work together in a good way (with respect to load-balance and locality). This effort is translated to programmer time, line count, and code complexity. Sometimes, a program benefits from grouping because it may allow saving duplicate work. If the blocks of work are very small, this grouping serves as thread coarsening. However, in some cases, by incurring extra work, it can even result in a less efficient program.

We evaluate the effects of task composition on each of three programs (mmult, convolution and dag) by comparing two versions – XMT and Traditional. The traditional version always spawns exactly one thread for each TCU, and a loop is added to the thread body to span through all the blocks of work that are assigned to the thread (Table 1).

Table 1. Effects of task decomposition on programming of parallel dot product computation.

XMT	Traditional
spawn(N*N,0);	spawn(tcus,0);
{	{

```
                                      lb =N*N*TID/tcus;
                                      ub =N*N*(TID+1)/tcus;
                                      for(m=lb;m<ub;m++){
   x = C[0][TID];                        x = C[0][m];
   i = TID/N; j = TID%N;                 I = m/N; j = m%N;
   for (k=0; k<N; k++){                  for (k=0;k<N;k++){
      x += A[i][k]*B[k][j];                 x += A[i][k]*B[k][j];
   }                                     }
   C[0][TID] = x;                        C[0][m] = x;
                                      }
}                                     }
join();                               join();
```

Note that even when the entire task of assignment involves only the few source lines (in bold font), we may still get up to 30% increase in length of code, in some cases accompanied with a decrease in performance.

We now examine the experimental results for the three programs (Figure 1). For both matrix multiplication and 2-D image convolution, the XMT version spawns a thread for each entry, while the traditional version clusters the entries, and spawns a thread for each cluster. A more irregular computation, the third program finds maximum paths in a DAG. The XMT version spawns a thread for each node, while in the traditional version each thread handles a cluster of nodes. (Note that we choose to show here the "xmt-sync" variant, as it is the closest to traditional version, though not the most efficient. Details on this and other DAG implementations appear in section 5.3.)

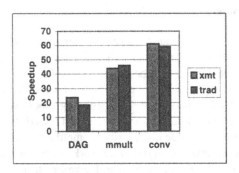

Fig. 1. Effects of no task assignment on performance. Speedups of parallel versions over the serial version, running on 64 TCUs.

For mmult and convolution, both versions achieve similar speedups. The traditional mmult is able to amortize some duplicate work, while the XMT version of convolution takes the lead by avoiding some task assignment overhead. For DAG, load balancing issues come into play, penalizing static assignment in the traditional version. For 16 TCUs, costs due to load imbalance constitute 35% of the traditional program running time versus 16% for XMT.

5.2   Fine-grained Parallelism

The XMT programming methodology encourages the programmer to express any parallelism, regardless of how fine-grained it may be. The low overheads involved in emulating the threads allow this fine-grained parallelism to be competitive. However, despite the efficient implementation, extremely fine-grained programs can benefit from coarsening as it may allow to 1) exploit spatial locality, and 2) reduce duplicate work; however, these opportunities occur only in regular codes, such as scientific array-based computations, where it is also easy to automatically detect and optimize. By grouping consecutive threads, clustering exploits spatial locality, and allows the programmer to ignore granularity and task assignment considerations, which are otherwise relevant.

The XMT compiler detects cases where the length of a thread is sufficiently small (such that the thread overhead constitutes a significant enough portion of the thread). This parameter is evaluated at compile time, using SUIF's static performance estimation utility. The compiler then automatically transforms the spawn block such that fewer but longer threads are used. In the results we report here, we use grain size as big as possible, where the number of clustered threads is fixed to the number of TCUS. A few unclustered-threads are reserved at the tail of the spawn. Tuning this value can reduce the load imbalance cost.

To evaluate the effects of granularity on performance, we use the following three programs: LU, a linear algebra program that computes lower-upper matrix factorization. Jacobi, a 2-D PDE kernel, and dbscan – a database kernel that emulates an SQL query on a non-indexed attributes relation. We compare several versions for each: 1) fine-grained: each thread handles one entry, 2) by-row: each thread computes an entire row, 3) clustered: the fine-grained version coarsened by the XMT compiler, 4) traditional: by-row, with the work assigned to processors (as described in the section above). (For dbscan we compare only 3 versions - fine-grained, clustered, and traditional).

All three programs demonstrate the same behavior (Figure 2). For the smallest problem sizes, the best speedups are achieved by the fine-grained version, where the coarsest version (traditional) gets the lowest speedups. As the problem size increases, the coarser versions beat the fine-grained one, while the by-row version is the fastest version. Though the advantage that the fine-grained versions demonstrate for the smaller sizes is not decisive, it suggests that in the general case, algorithms for more irregular applications may benefit. As an example, in section 5.4 we describe how our implementations of radixsort and quicksort take advantage of fine-grained parallelism.

For more regular applications however, the XMT compiler can make fine-grained programs competitive with the coarse-grained versions by automatically clustering the parallel regions. This allows the programmer to ignore granularity considerations, and directly write the easier fine-grained version.

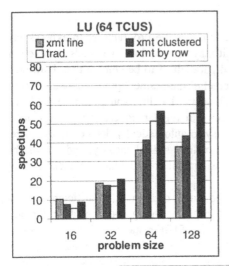

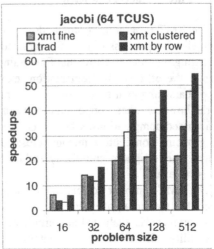

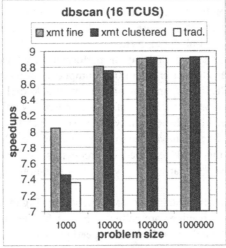

Fig. 2. Effects of granularity on performance. Speedups of parallel versions over the serial version.

5.3 Synchronization: Scalable Mechanisms and Asynchronous Algorithms

Traditional parallel programs typically use locks and barriers for synchronization. As we will demonstrate, these synchronization mechanisms can be efficiently supported in XMT. However, typically XMT addresses synchronization in a manner that minimizes busy-waiting. In many cases, the parallel prefix sum operation can be used instead of a lock, and the join serves as a barrier. Alternatively, an XMT methodology can often suggest an entirely different algorithm. We examine these alternatives with two representative programs, dot and DAG. We show results for relatively small input sizes, where the relative costs of the various techniques are easily seen. While differences tend to be less dramatic with larger workloads, the same trends are evident.

Dot product is an example of a common reduction task. We compare the following versions for dot:

1. XMT-algorithmic-style programs, using a binary tree structure for no-busy-wait synchronization [15]. We wrote two programs in this style, one propagates values up the tree in a synchronous fashion, involving a spawn and join for each layer of the tree ("xmt-sync"). The other version propagates the values in an asynchronous fashion, involving only one spawn-join block, within which the threads advance as far as they can ("xmt-async").

2. Traditional style programs, in the sense that the problem is decomposed in a coarse-grained fashion between the processing units. However, XMT utilities are used for synchronization. In the "x_trad-ps" version, the TCUs update the global dot product atomically with their portion of the computation using the parallel prefix–sum mechanism, instead of locking. In the "x_trad-join" version, after all the TCUs have completed computing their portion, they join, instead of using a barrier, and the global dot product is computed serially after the join by a single TCU.

3. Traditional style programs, using busy-wait synchronization. The "trad_PRlock" uses the most efficient but somewhat specialized parallel prefix-sum operation, while "trad_memlock" uses a less scalable but more general fetch-and-add mechanism. "trad-barr" uses a barrier.

The general trend is that programs using non-XMT synchronization scale poorly with the number of TCUs compared to the others (Figure 3). The exception is the "xmt-async" version due to the amount of storage and extra work that it involves.

This trend in synchronization primitive scalability is further reinforced when examining the performance of different versions for the DAG program. In addition, the irregular nature of the computation makes it a good candidate for a less synchronous programming style. Especially with sparser graphs, asynchronous programs should excel by enabling parallelism as soon as it is discovered. We compare the following versions [15]:

1. XMT style, synchronous fashion: "sync". A thread is spawned for each node with in-degree 0. Each thread steps through the outgoing edges of the node, and decrements the in-degree of the sink nodes. After a join, threads are spawned for newly in-degree 0 nodes. The process is repeated until all nodes are processed.

2. Traditional style. These versions are based on the "sync" version, adding the necessary decomposition. One program uses the prefix-sum as a synchronization mechanism ("trad"), and another uses locks instead ("trad-lock").

3. XMT style, asynchronous fashion: "async-node" and "async-edge". The async-node version spawns a thread for every node as in "sync". Whenever a thread decrements the in-degree of a sink node to zero, it forks a thread to process that node. Async-edge is similar, but a thread processing a node forks a thread to pro-

cess every outgoing edge. Async-edge is the finest-grain, least-synchronous of the versions.

As expected, the more synchronous the algorithm is, the worse it scales with the number of TCUs. This trend can be seen by comparing the relative performance of async-edge, async-node, and sync (Figure 3).

We again see the effect of synchronization mechanism overhead on scalability. The relative performance of trad and trad-lock illustrates the superiority of prefix-sum compared to traditional busy-wait locking.

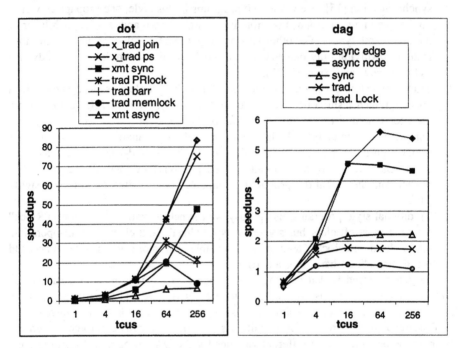

Fig. 3. Synchronization options in dot (4096 elements), and dag (100 nodes, 473 edges). Speed-ups of parallel versions over the serial version on increasing number of TCUs.

5.4 Two Case Studies

In this section we provide two examples of how the combination of features in XMT enables new approaches that outperform more traditional algorithms.

Radix. This integer sort consists of the stable radix sort routine that is applied iteratively to each "digit" of the input until fully sorted. For every value a digit might take, we say there is a bin for the key to go in. By counting the number of keys for each bin, we can determine a final rank for each bin.

SPLASH radix uses the common parallel algorithm of [1]. It operates with P processors on N input keys. Each processor is assigned a continuous partition of N/P keys, and locally computes bin counts from its own partition. Since each processor has its own set of bin counters, a global ranking operation must be performed. A binary tree of bin counter arrays is formed. Each processor ranks its bins locally and then either sums results from other processors further up the tree, or waits for partial sums to be propagated back down the tree. Finally, with globally ranked bins, each processor can copy each of its keys in sequence to the output array.

One of the hurdles to scalability is that each processor needs its own set of bin counters. The more processors that are applied to a problem, the more time must be spent doing global ranking. This effectively limits the P for the SPLASH radix. In an XMT style program, significantly more parallelism can be expressed.

Due to the need to preserve equal-key order, we are limited to the P sequential threads to serially copy keys within individual partitions. However, the bin counting step can be much more fine-grained. Provided that threads cope with simultaneous access to the same bin counter (e.g. with the prefix-sum primitive), it is possible to spawn a separate thread for each key of input.

The global ranking step can also be finer-grained. SPLASH operates with a granularity of an entire bin counter array. The XMT approach does not insist that the programmer wrestle with data locality. In this light, the global ranking step can be considered to be a single, large prefix-sum operation, where the inputs are the interleaved bin counters from all the processors. It is then a simple matter to apply a fine-grained binary-tree parallel prefix algorithm.

There is certainly a cost to the more fine-grained algorithm. Without automated coarsening of the XMT threads, the coarser-threaded bin counting clearly has the work advantage. With 1 TCU, the XMT algorithm performs nearly twice the work of SPLASH (Figure 4). However, with 16 TCUs, the SPLASH algorithm is already doing worse than it did with 4 TCUs. In contrast, the finer-grained program easily scales to 16 TCUs. (Note that these results are for an input of 16K keys, while SPLASH defaults to 256K keys.)

Quicksort. Quicksort provides another simple illustration of how XMT might be able to express parallelism that is traditionally neglected. A classic example of the divide-and-conquer approach, quicksort is a recursive sort using pivots.

The traditional parallel quicksort follows this divide-and-conquer approach. After splitting a partition, a thread forks a new thread to sort the right side, and does the left side itself.

In XMT, the forking need not stop when the full machine parallelism is reached. Newly created partitions are queued up, and automatically assigned to threads without complicated programmer intervention. This dynamic load balancing is particularly useful for handling the unpredictable partitioning of quicksort.

This approach is still less than ideal. At the beginning of the program, only one thread is active. A machine can not be utilized fully until enough partitions have been created. Unfortunately, the partitions encountered at the start of the computation are the largest and therefore take the longest time to split.

A fine-grained XMT program can parallelize the partition step. A thread is spawned for each element of the partition. Two counters – "left" and "right" are maintained. The left (right) counter keeps track of the number of elements which value is less (greater) than the pivot, and are thus copied to the left (right) partition. A prefix-sum to either the left counter or the right counter determines the output rank of the element.

Since the latter method requires synchronization at each partition, we do not wish to use this algorithm throughout the program. The optimal solution is to start with the fine-grained, synchronous parallel partitioning algorithm, and then switch to the traditional divide-and-conquer when a sufficient number of partitions are available. With a 64 TCU configuration operating on 16,384 elements, this hybrid approach is more than twice as fast as the traditional approach.

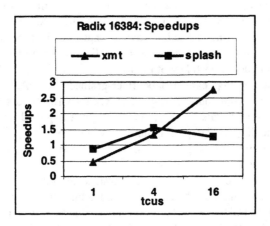

Fig. 4. XMT vs. SPLASH implementation for radix sort. Speedups of parallel versions over the serial version on increasing number of TCUs.

6 Related Work

Recent work on comparing different parallel programming models [9], [5], [12], [4], typically focuses on the shared-memory and message-passing programming models on multiprocessor systems. Our work attempts to examine parallel programming with respect to the different assumptions implied by an on-chip environment.

Various other projects explore on-chip parallel architectures: CMP [10], Multiscalar [8], SMT [13]. The current paper is targeted toward exploring shared-memory parallel algorithms as applied to scalable on-chip architecture. Note that XMT, with the parallel prefix-sum for example, aspires to scale up to much higher levels of parallelism than other single-chip multithreaded architectures consider currently. Tile based architectures, such as MIT's Raw [16], also expect to scale to high levels of parallelism. However, Raw utilizes a message-passing model rather than the shared-memory model of XMT. In addition, Raw heavily relies on compiler technology to manage data distribution and movements between tiles. As such, it is much easier to program for the XMT architecture, and it is also expected to address a wider range of applications.

MIT's Cilk [7] provides a multi-threaded programming interface and execution model. There are two important differences in scope. First, since Cilk is targeted at compatibility with existing SMP machines, load balancing in software is an important element of the project. XMT requires hardware support to bind virtual threads to thread control units (TCUs) exactly as the TCUs become available. The low-overhead of XMT is designed to be applicable to a much broader range of applications. Second, Cilk presents a programming model that tries to match very closely standard serial programming constructs, where forking a thread takes the form of a function call. While XMT also bases its programming model on standard C, the programmer is expected to rethink the way parallelism is expressed. The wide-spawn capabilities and prefix-sum primitive are present to support the many algorithms targeted to the PRAM model.

7 Conclusion

This paper presented features of XMT, a parallel programming model designed for exploiting on-chip parallelism. With prototype compiler and architecture simulator, we studied XMT programming in areas where parallel computing has underperformed in the past: very fine-grained parallelism; smaller problem sizes; and unpredictable, irregular computations.

XMT features encourage programmers to write high level programs with more fine-grained parallelism, without worrying about assigning threads to processors. We found the XMT architecture and compiler can usually support this simple fine-grained programming style with little loss in performance for on-chip multiprocessors. Thread coarsening is necessary in some cases, but can usually be automatically applied by the XMT compiler. After thread coarsening, lack of explicit task assignment has only slight effect on performance for the XMT architecture.

When overheads are low enough so that parallelism can be leveraged even for small inputs, many more tasks can potentially be sped up.

The flexible programming style also encourages the development of new algorithms to take advantage of properties of on-chip parallelism. We demonstrated that XMT is especially useful for more advanced applications with dynamic, irregular access patterns.

References

1. G. E. Blelloch et. al, "A Comparison of Sorting Algorithms for the Connection Machine CM-2," Symposium on Parallel Algorithms and Architectures, pp. 3-16, July 1991.
2. D. Burger and T. M. Austin, "The SimpleScalar Tool Set, Version 2.0," Tech. Report CS-1342, University of Wisconsin-Madison, June 1997.
3. E. Berkovich, J. Nuzman, M. Franklin, B. Jacob, U. Vishkin, "XMT-M: A scalable decentralized processor," UMIACS TR 99-55, September 1999.
4. B.L. Chamberlain, S.J. Deitz, L. Snyder, "A Comparative Study of the NAS MG Benchmark across Parallel Languages and Architectures," Proc. of Supercomputing (SC), 2000.
5. F. Cappello, D. Etiemble, "MPI versus MPI+OpenMP on the IBM SP for the NAS Benchmarks," Proc. of Supercomputing (SC), 2000.
6. S. Dascal and U. Vishkin, "Experiments with List Ranking on Explicit Multi-Threaded (XMT) Instruction Parallelism," Proc. 3rd Workshop on Algorithms Engineering (WAE-99), July 1999, London, U.K.
7. M. Frigo, C. Leiserson, K. Randall, "The Implementation of the Cilk-5 Multi-threaded Language," Proc. of the 1998 ACM SIGPLAN Conference on Programming Language Design and Implementation (PLDI), 1998.
8. M. Franklin, "The Multiscalar Architecture," Ph.D. thesis. Technical Report TR 1196, Computer Sciences Department, University of Wisconsin-Madison, December 1993.
9. D.S.Henty, "Performance of Hybrid Message-Passing and Shared-Memory Parallelism for Discrete Element Modeling," Proc. of Supercomputing (SC), 2000.
10. L. Hammond, B. Nayfeh, and K. Olukotun, "A Single-Chip Multiprocessor," IEEE Computer, Vol. 30, pp. 79-85, September 1997.
11. D. Naishlos, J. Nuzman, C.-W. Tseng, and U. Vishkin, "Evaluating Multi-threading in the Prototype XMT Environment," In Proc. 4th Workshop on Multi-Threaded Execution, Architecture and Compliation (MTEAC2000), December 2000
12. H. Shan, J.P. Singh, L. Oliker, R. Biswas, "A Comparison of Three Programming Models for Adaptive Aplications on the Origin2000," Proc. of Supercomputing (SC), 2000.
13. D. Tullsen, J. Lo, S. Eggers, H. Levy, "Supporting Fine-Grained Synchronization on a Simultaneous Multi-threading Processor," Proc. of the 5th International Symposium on High Performance Computer Architecture, 1999.
14. U. Vishkin, S. Dascal, E. Berkovich, and J. Nuzman, "Explicit Multi-threaded (XMT) Bridging Models for Instruction Parallelism," Proc. 10th ACM Symposium on Parallel Algorithms and Architectures (SPAA), pp. 140-151, 1998.
15. U. Vishkin, "A No-Busy-Wait Balanced Tree Parallel Algorithmic Paradigm," Proc. 12th ACM Symposium on Parallel Algorithms and Architectures (SPAA), 2000.
16. E. Waingold, M. Tayor, D. Srikrishna, V. Sarkar, W. Lee, V. Lee, J. Kim, M. Frank, P. Finch, R. Barua, J. Babb, S. Amarasinghe, and A. Agarwal, "Baring It All to Software: Raw Machines," IEEE Computer, Vol. 30, pp. 86-93, September 1997.
17. R. Wilson et al, "SUIF: An Infrastructure for Research on Parallelizing and Optimizing Compilers," ACM SIGPLAN Notices, v. 29, n. 12, pp. 31-37, December 1994.

DEPICT: A Topology-Based Debugger for MPI Programs

Simon Huband and Chris McDonald

The University of Western Australia
Department of Computer Science & Software Engineering
Nedlands, Western Australia 6907, Australia
{huey, chris}@cs.uwa.edu.au

Abstract. Most parallel programs use regular topologies to support their computation. Since they define the relationship between processes, process topologies present an excellent opportunity for debugging. The primary benefit is that patterns of expected behaviour can be abstracted and identified, and unexpected behaviour reported.

However, topology support is inadequate in many environments, including the popular Message Passing Interface (MPI). Programmers typically implement topology support themselves, increasing the possibility of introducing errors. Moreover, debugger support that exploits topological information is lacking.

We have undertaken to develop a debugger that exploits topological information. This paper presents DEPICT (DEbugger of Parallel but Inconsistent Communication Traces), a (preliminary) topology-based debugger for MPI. Currently, DEPICT presents high-level visualisations of parallel program communication behaviour, where logically similar processes are clearly indicated in a manner that allows the programmer insight into overall program behaviour. To assist in understanding unexpected behaviour, DEPICT allows programmers to investigate the observed semantic differences between processes.

1   Introduction

The parallel programming paradigm is powerful in that it allows scientists and engineers to address a variety of computationally expensive problems. The hardware employed to address such computationally expensive problems ranges between dedicated supercomputers and distributed memory multi-processors, to the less expensive collection of powerful off-the-shelf personal computers connected via high-speed networks (workstation clusters).

A variety environments support the development of parallel programs under the given hardware environment. One prominent example is the language extensions offered by the Message Passing Interface (MPI) [13], which allows programmers to enjoy one of the most popular communication paradigms today: message passing.

The computing model supported by message passing environments is both simple and very general, and accommodates a wide variety of application program structures. The programming interfaces are deliberately straightforward, thus permitting simple program structures to be implemented in an intuitive manner. The user writes an application as a collection of cooperating tasks. Tasks access message passing resources through a library of standard interface routines. These routines support the initiation and termination of tasks, as well as communication and synchronization between tasks. Communication constructs include those for sending and receiving data structures as well as high-level primitives such as message broadcast, synchronization, and some global arithmetic operations.

Despite its popularity, MPI is not particularly elegant at expressing many parallel problems. It is necessary to specify the destination of messages using a task descriptor (rank) which uniquely identifies the task to receive the message. This directly contrasts with the method that most parallel programs use to describe their communication patterns. Many parallel algorithms employ one or more standard process topologies, within which the physical relationship between tasks is specified, and the communication patterns are implied. For example, when computing solutions to problems whose data forms a two dimensional matrix, or mesh, it is natural for each node to communicate with its immediate neighbours in its row or column. When these problems are formulated as algorithms, it is natural to specify the destination of each message in terms of the primary compass directions, rather than using an abstract identifier bearing no logical resemblance to the problem being solved.

A number of standard process topologies are well identified [12]. These include pipelines, rings, hypercubes, and trees. However, traditional MPI does not allow problems to be expressed in terms of these logical communication patterns [7]. Recent research by Kazemi and McDonald [8] largely addresses this issue; extensions to MPI (and the Parallel Virtual Machine (PVM) [2]) are provided that support the specification of logical communication patterns by providing symbolic constants such as SEND_TO_NORTH, BROADCAST_TO_ROW, and RECV_FROM_DOWNSTREAM.

A number of factors complicate parallel program debugging [1]. One difficult area involves detecting or locating communication errors. Concurrently executing processes complicates program understanding, and can obscure the point of origin of errors. Namely, errors can originate in processes other than the process showing the symptoms of the error. Unfortunately, current debugging techniques are too fine-grained, and focus too much on the source code. Often programmers must resort to examining traces of inter-process communication pairings, or attempt to instrument their code with traditional console I/O (ala printf() in C programs). Both techniques are flawed. Program traces easily overload programmers (and communication networks) with information; often there are large volumes of messages, and programmers are limited to identifying processes using numeric values. Additional tools are often required to make any degree of sense of traces. With console I/O, not only can too much information be produced, but there is a greater degree of program intrusion, which leads to the probe effect, a serious issue in non-deterministic parallel programs: changing a program's timing can result in different behaviour, and therefore the manifestation of different errors. Minimising the probe effect is important.

The lack of explicit topology support constrains the way we think about debugging parallel programs. Topological knowledge is a valuable debugging aid, especially with respect to program understanding. For example, topological knowledge can be used to identify misdirected messages. It can also be used to better summarise process behaviour. In particular, processes can refer to each other via logical descriptors, such as NORTH, instead of numeric descriptors. Such knowledge provides a powerful mechanism whereby the behaviour of processes can be correlated, and the detection of patterns of events made. Without assistance, humans find it difficult to identify patterns of events from traces, and even from event animations. Topological knowledge is also important if a topologically consistent display of the processes is expected. Although generic parallel debugging visualisations could be applied, without knowledge of the topology, display scalability becomes a serious issue.

Despite the assistance a topology-based debugger can provide, to our knowledge there are no such debuggers for MPI. We have undertaken to develop such a debugger. This paper presents a preliminary post-mortem trace-based topological debugger for MPI, DEPICT (DEbugger of Parallel but Inconsistent Communication Traces). We note that although our work focuses on MPI, the concepts are extendible to other environments, such as PVM.

Debuggers are often used as a last resort. The programmer usually believes their code is correct, so they cannot understand why their program is in error. Debuggers are employed to help locate where a program does not act as the programmer expects it to. A debugger can only try to correct a programmer's incorrect perception of their program's behaviour. Debuggers cannot be expected to explain why an error is present, but they are expected to provide meaningful information that the programmer can analyse and act upon.

DEPICT provides meaningful debugging information by exploiting the fact that topology-based programs are expected to exhibit regular, periodic communication patterns. Often one or more subsets of correct topology-based programs exhibit similar behaviour. By visualising equivalent classes of processes, DEPICT provides high-level views of program communication behaviour. DEPICT does not just present the trace graphically, it analyses and abstracts it further, making its representation closer to the actual program constructs, and thereby more useful.

The programmer can compare DEPICT's output against their mental view of the program, where differences identify regions of concern. Since a programmer is familiar with their own code, they can correlate the geographical location of anomalies against the source code, which suggests the probable source of error.

In the next section we discuss material related to our research. In Sect. 3 we describe in detail the makeup of DEPICT. Examples using DEPICT are given in Sect. 4, after which, in Sect. 5, we conclude our paper.

2 Related Work

Processes in MPI are identified by their numeric rank, where there is no requirement that programmers use ranks in a logical or natural manner. Consequently, by analysing only trace files, the position of processes within topologies is not necessarily clear. In suggesting the topology-based debugging approach, Huband and McDonald [6] identify and investigate the "topology identification" issue.

Huband and McDonald indicate that trace files provide sufficient information for the identification of process topologies, given potentially random task descriptors, and the possibility of errors. They suggest using graph distance measures as a means of identifying a topology, where, given a set of ideal candidate topologies, the idea is to find mappings of processes into each candidate such that the number of mismatched edges is minimised in each case. The minimum number of mismatched edges is the distance. The candidate with least distance to the actual program topology is suggested as the intended topology.

However, determining optimum mappings of processes is, in degenerate cases, an NP-hard problem. In the case of topologies, as more errors are introduced, the more difficult the problem becomes. Conversely, in the absence of errors, identifying topologies is trivial. Huband and McDonald demonstrate that even in the presence of errors, by using topology-specific properties where necessary, topology identification is tractable.

At present we make the reasonable assumption that MPI ranks are used naturally, not randomly. This has allowed us to concentrate on other aspects of DEPICT, instead of concerning ourselves with worst-case scenarios.

DEPICT is not the first tool to exploit process topologies. The X-based Compound Event Recognition Tool (XCERT) [15] is a topology-based debugger initially designed for the Fujitsu AP1000. XCERT, which only supports the mesh topology, accepts LERP logs by way of input, analyses them, and simplifies process traces by introducing compound events and count tags. Compound events span only one process and consist of atomic and possibly other compound events. Count tags represent the number of times a particular compound event is repeated in the trace for a process at the given position.

XCERT uses a statistical approach to determine compound events, where preference is assigned to identifying larger sequences of compound events before smaller sequences. Once compound events are identified, they are substituted across all process traces. Using reduced task signatures, or task traces using compound events where the count tag is ignored, XCERT identifies equivalence classes of processes, where two processes belong to the same equivalence class if their reduced signature is identical. XCERT displays the equivalence classes, allowing the user to see the observed behaviour of their program.

Although they are for different platforms, some aspects of XCERT are similar to DEPICT. However, DEPICT employs a number of more advanced techniques, including:

- DEPICT employs an algorithmic approach rather than a statistical approach,

- DEPICT allows for a combination of absolute and relative addressing schemes instead of requiring the use of one or the other, and
- DEPICT provides facility for identifying the differences between two process execution histories (DEPICT's functionality is described in Sect. 3).

Belvedere [5] is a post-mortem debugger where users define abstract events (for example, "when all even rows swap values") that typically span multiple processes. Belvedere animates identified events, where individual low-level participating events are animated simultaneously.

Ariadne [11] is another post-mortem tool, where users specify the behaviour expected of their program. Ariadne attempts to match the specified behaviour against the actual behaviour. The resulting match (or mismatch) is displayed using the Ariadne Visualisation Engine.

Whilst both Belvedere and Ariadne provide powerful facilities, they require the user to specify in advance the patterns appropriate to their program. However, users tend to be reluctant to use debuggers that require such a learning curve. In addition, whilst programmers can verify the behaviour of their programs against presented models, not all are capable of clearly specifying behaviour.

ATEMPT (A Tool for Event ManiPulaTion) [10], a part of the MAD (Monitoring And Debugging) environment [9], presents an alternative approach to parallel program debugging. ATEMPT uses a partially ordered (in time) space-time diagram to depict a program's communication history. Processes are represented by horizontal lines, and the interaction between processes is shown by directed lines. ATEMPT provides facilities to detect simple communication errors, such as events with different message lengths, isolated events, or race conditions. ATEMPT also provides some mechanisms to abstract the display on a process and event level. Whilst ATEMPT provides some useful functionality for the detection of errors, space-time diagrams can become cluttered and confusing (although ATEMPT's abstraction mechanisms alleviate this to some degree). Moreover, space-time diagrams do not exploit process topology information in that processes are not arranged in a toplogically consistent manner.

ParaGraph [3] is a post-mortem performance debugger that uses the same trace file format as DEPICT currently uses, the Portable Instrumented Communication Library (PICL) extension MPICL (see Sect. 3). ParaGraph provides various displays and animations to assist the performance analysis and tuning of parallel programs, including some that visually arrange processes according to a user selected topology.

There are numerous other parallel debugging programs and approaches designed for MPI and other environments, including, among others, the Annai tool environment [17], and the p2d2 source code debugger [4].

3 DEPICT

DEPICT is a high-level, post-mortem trace-based debugger written in C++ with a Tcl/Tk graphical front-end for use with topology-based MPI programs.

DEPICT's two key aspects include its visualisation of program behaviour, and its process comparison utility. The program visualisation allows programmers to gauge the correctness of overall program communication structures, and the comparison utility allows programmers to investigate the difference in behaviour exhibited by different processes. DEPICT does not analyse the program at the source code level, but instead analyses the observable semantics as traced. Examples of DEPICT's appearance can be found in Sect. 4.

DEPICT's components are described below. They include the trace file interpreter, the topology handler, the group identifier, and the graphical user interface. A number of components are still being enhanced, in particular the topology handler and the graphical user interface.

3.1   Trace File Interpreter

MPI programs that are analysed by DEPICT are currently traced using MPI-CL [16], the output of which is read by the trace file interpreter post-mortem. There are several factors contributing to our decision to use MPICL, namely:

– MPICL's trace format supports our requirements,
– MPICL's trace format is human readable ASCII text, simplifying the design of the trace file interpreter, and
– MPICL uses MPI's profiling interface, making it portable to a number MPI implementations.

Unfortunately, MPICL is not entirely suitable. MPICL was originally designed for post-mortem performance analysis, not post-mortem error debugging. Consequently, MPICL only produces complete trace files when all processes successfully execute MPI_Finalize. Clearly this is unsatisfactory since it excludes the analysis of programs that fail catastrophically mid-way through execution. As such we are implementing our own robust profiling library as an alternative to MPICL.

3.2   Topology Handler

The topology handler is responsible for determining the particulars of program topologies, given the point-to-point communication trace information (as provided by the trace file interpreter) and the topology name as provided by the programmer. Collective communication events are not currently used in topology analysis.

Using the available data, the topology handler determines the dimensions of the specified topology, identifies the process ordering scheme used (such as row-major for a mesh), and provides an abstract interface for the group identifier and the graphical user interface.

For its first two roles, the topology handler makes the reasonable assumption that process rank numbers are used in a logically consistent manner. For example, in a row-major mesh, process rank 0 always corresponds to the first row and column. Note that for performance reasons routines such as MPI_Cart_create provide options to allow reordering of process rank numbers. Consequently, traced MPI_COMM_WORLD ranks could look as though they were used haphazardly. We note that MPI's profiling interface could trivially be used to disable such optimisation features.

As part of providing an abstract interface for the next two components, the topology handler converts the destination and source ranks of SENDs and RECVs respectively so that they are represented using relative addresses. For example, a process in a mesh could be said to send a message to the process located "two rows north, one row east" instead of stating the destination process' rank explicitly. Since it is not clear whether the programmer is using a relative or absolute addressing scheme (or a combination), no assumption is made, and the absolute addresses are not discarded. Instead, on an event-by-event basis, DEPICT automatically deduces whether relative or absolute addresses are used.

DEPICT currently supports the mesh and torus topologies, where processes appear in row-major order.

3.3 Group Identifier

The group identifier is responsible for determining sets of processes that exhibit logically identical or similar behaviour. Although not described, it is in this component where point-to-point communication events are determined to use either absolute or relative addresses, or if it remains unclear, possibly both.

First, the input is split into separate trace streams, one for each process. Cycles of repeated patterns of events, or compound events, are then identified; compound events do not span multiple processes. Subsequently, process traces are reconstructed where patterns of repeated behaviour are represented using low-level loop-like constructs.

Note that although similar, the use of loop-like constructs and compound events does not necessarily reflect the actual loop at source code level constructs of the program. We are not aware of any trace file format that would guarantee the correct identification of actual loop constructs.

The group identifier classifies processes into groups where two processes are assigned the same group if and only if their reconstructed traces are similar. Two traces are similar if they appear identical when the number of loop-like construct iterations (and sub-loops, and so on) are ignored. Therefore, processes executing instructions a variable number of times based upon their position in the topology (which occurs in "wavefront" algorithms for example) are assigned the same group.

The group identifier does not make allowances for boundary effects. For example, only the northernmost row of processes in a mesh cannot send messages north. Consequently, the northernmost mesh processes would typically exhibit different communication patterns to the remaining processes. A similar observation can be made for the westernmost, easternmost, and southernmost mesh processes. Whilst the group identifier does not allow for boundary effects, it may be desirable to do so in order to see, for example, how a torus approximates a mesh.

The group identifier's method of classifying processes is only helpful when a program executes consistent, regular patterns. This is not always the case, since the communication of some programs vary according to the input data (data-driven communication patterns), and look irregular from external (trace-based) perspectives; messages may be selectively directed to neighbouring processes according to the input data in a manner that is not clearly regular. In addition, programs that use "tricks" to optimise communication performance may also compromise the group identifier. Even so, the regular communication patterns employed by most parallel programs are well supported by our approach.

3.4 Graphical User Interface

The graphical user interface uses the abstract interface provided by the topology handler to display processes in a manner consistent with the identified topology. In addition, equivalent processes are displayed in the same colour, and vice versa. To account for large topologies, techniques for scaling the display are currently under investigation.

This program behaviour visualisation allows the programmer immediate insight into the overall characteristics of the program. If the view provided is dissimilar to the programmer's mental model, and assuming the mental model is correct, then there must be a communication error present. The inconsistent processes indicate where in the source code the programmer could first look for errors.

In addition, the user can request a textual display of the execution history for a single group. This is represented using the derived low-level loop-like constructs.

The graphical user interface also provides a comparison utility, where the changes required to convert one group trace to another are identified. The display is similar to the single group display, but blue text represents event insertion, and red text represents event deletion. The comparison utility assists in identifying how particular processes behave differently. Section 4 includes an example of this display.

4 Examples of Use

We have tested DEPICT against a number of algorithms, each with deliberately introduced errors. Three of the tests are presented here: a matrix multiplication algorithm for the torus, a matrix multiplication algorithm for the mesh, and a linear sort algorithm for the linear array (one-dimensional mesh). The algorithms are described elsewhere [14].

Due to MPICL's constraints, errors are such that all programs exit normally. Instead of failing catastrophically, each program returns incorrect results. In most cases the introduced errors are subtle and easy to overlook.

As DEPICT's output is in colour, and this paper is not, screen shots have been manually annotated for clarity.

4.1 Matrix Multiply for the Torus

This algorithm was executed on an 6×6 (logical) torus. Every process is expected to exhibit identical behaviour. However, a missing `else` statement causes the easternmost column of processes to ignore incoming messages from the westernmost column.

DEPICT's display (Fig. 1) highlights the presence of the error: the easternmost column of processes are in their own group, indicating different behaviour. Using DEPICT's comparison query reveals the absent `MPI_Recv` (Fig. 2).

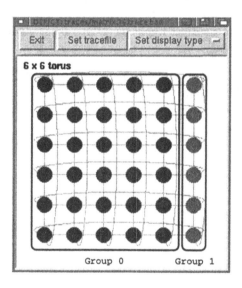

Fig. 1. Incorrect matrix multiply, torus

4.2 Matrix Multiply for the Mesh

Like the algorithm for the torus, this algorithm was tested on an 6×6 mesh. This algorithm was implemented since it exhibits a variety of different process behaviours, where:

- the northwest quadrant does not participate,
- the northeast and southwest quadrants send and receive messages in the vertical and horizontal directions respectively, and
- the southeast quadrant sends and receives messages in both the vertical and horizontal directions.

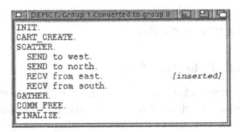

Fig. 2. Comparing group 1 to group 0

Process position in the topology also dictates the number of times certain loops are executed. Boundary processes behave differently to the norm. Figure 3 shows DEPICT's output for a correct implementation of this algorithm.

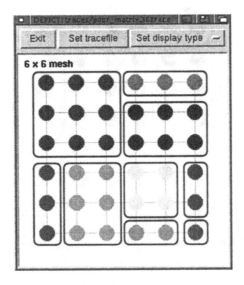

Fig. 3. Correct matrix multiply, mesh

The error introduced to this algorithm involves two MPI_Recv statements that receive messages from MPI_ANY_SOURCE, in a situation where messages that should be treated differently are expected from two different sources. In our experience, this kind of error is frequently made by novice programmers. The incorrect code corresponds to the southeast quadrant of the mesh.

Upon analysing the trace output, DEPICT presents the display shown in Fig. 4. It is clear that the southeast quadrant is not executing regularly. Displaying the trace for the southeastern processes reveals a relatively confusing jumble of events; since the execution history is erratic, DEPICT cannot concisely summarise the behaviour.

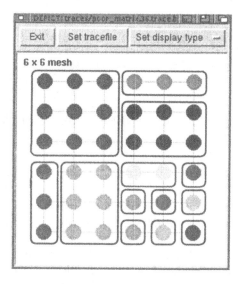

Fig. 4. Incorrect matrix multiply, mesh

In this example, DEPICT correctly shows that the code governing the southeast quadrant of the program is in error.

4.3 Linear Sort

Our implementation of the linear sort algorithm has been tested on the 1 × 18 mesh. In a correct implementation of the linear sort algorithm, all but the easternmost and westernmost processes exhibit identical behaviour. The number of times the main loop is iterated decreases the further east a process is located.

Our implementation of the linear sort algorithm is incorrect in that the main loop iterates one less than it should, as caused by an incorrect bound.

As can be seen in Fig. 5, the second last process is not behaving the same as the other inner processes. Investigation identifies that the final process is not executing the primary loop at all, and that the second last process executes the primary loop but once, when it should be executed twice. These provide clear indications of an error in the bound of the main loop.

This error only manifests itself for some types of input data, although DEPICT always highlights the inconsistency, even when the output is correct for the given input. This is because the communication patterns are modified by the error, even if the returned result is not. Since DEPICT analyses communication

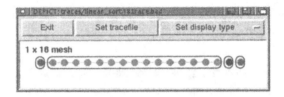

Fig. 5. Incorrect linear sort

patterns instead of program output, DEPICT will always identify these types of errors.

5 Conclusion

Topological knowledge is clearly useful for a (constrained) class of debugging purposes. In each of the tests, DEPICT provided insight regarding the source and type of error. Given none of the programs crashed, and the subtlety of the errors, a programmer could plausibly overlook such errors. Nonetheless, DEPICT clearly indicated the presence of errors, regardless of actual output, since the communication semantics were incorrect. DEPICT could easily be employed to verify the correctness of communication patterns for programs that seem otherwise correct.

We do not always expect the topological debugging approach to be useful. Programs that exhibit no regular communication structures are not analysed, and traditional errors, such as invalid memory references, are not addressed. We expect traditional errors to be handled by more traditional debuggers: DEPICT is a debugger aimed at the high-level observable semantics of programs, not low-level concerns, although existing tools could be incorporated.

DEPICT is still in preliminary development, although much of the groundwork has been implemented. Our goal is for a complete debugger that exploits topological information. To this end, we have not ruled out the possibility of including features available in other tools. For example, we could include the facility to check that all SENDs are matched by RECVs. At present, we are concentrating on developing new features unique to parallel debuggers.

6 Acknowledgements

This work was supported in part by an Australian Postgraduate Award scholarship. We are also grateful for the assistance provided by Dr. Amitava Datta.

References

[1] Wing Hong Cheung, James P. Black, and Eric Manning. A framework for distributed debugging. *IEEE Software*, 7(1):106–115, January 1990.

[2] Al Geist, Adam Beguelin, Jack Dongarra, Weicheng Jiang, Robert Manchek, and Vaidy Sunderam. PVM 3 user's guide and reference manual. Available from http://www.netlib.org/pvm3/ug.ps, September 1994.

[3] Michael T. Heath and Jennifer A. Etheridge. Visualizing the performance of parallel programs. *IEEE Software*, 8(5):29–39, September 1991.

[4] Robert Hood. The p2d2 project: building a portable distributed debugger. In *Proceedings of SPDT '96: SIGMETRICS Symposium on Parallel and Distributed Tools*, pages 127–136. ACM, 1996.

[5] Alfred A. Hough and Janice E. Cuny. Initial experiences with a pattern-oriented parallel debugger. *SIGPLAN Notices*, 24(1):195–205, January 1989.

[6] Simon Huband and Chris McDonald. Debugging parallel programs using incomplete information. In Rajkumar Buyya, Mark Baker, Ken Hawick, and Heath James, editors, *Proceedings. 1st IEEE Computer Society International Workshop on Cluster Computing*, pages 278–286. IEEE Computer Society, 1999.

[7] K. Kazemi and C. S. McDonald. Process topologies for the Parallel Virtual Machine. *Australian Computer Science Communications*, 20(1):43–56, 1998.

[8] K. Kazemi and C. S. McDonald. General virtual process topology support in both MPI and PVM. *Australian Computer Science Communications*, 21(4):199–210, 1999.

[9] D. Kranzlmüller, S. Grabner, and J. Volkert. Debugging with the MAD environment. *Parallel Computing*, 23(1–2):199–217, April 1997.

[10] Dieter Kranzlmüller, Siegfried Grabner, and Jens Volkert. Debugging massively parallel programs with ATEMPT. In H. Liddell, A. Colbrook, B. Hertzberger, and P. Sloot, editors, *High-performance Computing and Networking. International Conference and Exhibition HPCN EUROPE 1996. Proceedings*, pages 806–811. Springer-Verlag, 1996.

[11] Joydip Kundu and Janice E. Cuny. A scalable, visual interface for debugging with event-based behavioral abstraction. In *Proceedings. Frontiers '95. The Fifth Symposium on the Frontiers of Massively Parallel Computation*, pages 472–479. IEEE Computer Society Press, 1994.

[12] F. Thomson Leighton. *Introduction to Parallel Algorithms and Architectures: Arrays, Trees, Hypercubes*. Morgan Kaufmann Publishers, Inc., San Mateo, CA, 1992.

[13] Message Passing Interface Forum. MPI-2: extensions to the message-passing interface. Available from http://www.mpi-forum.org/docs/docs.html, July 1997.

[14] Russ Miller and Quentin F. Stout. *Parallel Algorithms for Regular Architectures: Meshes and Pyramids*, chapter 2, pages 45–88. The MIT Press, 1996.

[15] P. B. Thistlewaite and C. W. Johnson. Towards debugging and analysis tools for kilo-processor computers. *Fujitsu Scientific and Technical Journal*, 29(1):32–40, March 1993.

[16] Patrick H. Worley. MPICL 2.0 instrumentation library for MPI. Available from http://www.epm.ornl.gov/picl/.

[17] Brian J. N. Wylie and Akiyoshi Endo. Annai/PMA multi-level hierarchical parallel program performance engineering. In *Proceedings. First International Workshop on High-Level Programming Models and Supportive Environments (HIPS '96)*, pages 58–67. IEEE Computer Society Press, 1996.

Correcting Errors in Message Passing Systems

Jan B. Pedersen (matt@cs.ubc.ca)   Alan Wagner (wagner@cs.ubc.ca)

University of British Columbia
Vancouver, British Columbia
Canada

Abstract. *We present an algorithm for correcting communication errors using delivered and undelivered messages. It is used to suggest corrective measures to remove errors introduced by typographical errors in message passing systems like PVM and MPI. The paper focuses on the validity of the algorithm by proving that for a nontrivial number of errors the algorithm can suggest changes to correct the errors. The algorithm has been implemented as a tool in* Millipede *(M*ulti *L*evel *I*nteractive *P*arallel **D**ebugger*), which is a support environment developed to assist programmers to debug message passing programs at different abstraction levels.*

1   Introduction

Detecting and correcting communication errors in message passing programs is a difficult problem. According to C. M. Pancake [3] the time spent debugging is comparable to the time it takes to write the program initially. Even simple communication errors are difficult to debug in a parallel environment with multiple processes exchanging large numbers of messages. Although there are visualization tools [1,2] to help users visualize the communication patterns of parallel programs there are very few tools for detecting and correcting errors based on the user's source code.

In this paper we introduce an algorithm that finds the fewest number of changes necessary to transform a program that deadlocks due to a communication error to one that does not deadlock. The algorithm is directed towards the type of communication errors that occur because of typographical errors in send and receive calls used by message libraries like MPI and PVM and and not those due to incorrect protocols. The algorithm not only works for statically specified communication. It can also be applied when the sender/receiver is specified through an index into an array or by a function call. It is then the programmers job to go back and fix the array/function to return what the algorithm suggests. We assume that these errors are independent and infrequent. However, the effectiveness of the technique decreases as the number of errors increases. It is straightforward in the case of one error but clearly of little use when the number of errors approaches the number of processes in the system.

The majority of the paper is devoted to theoretically justifying the validity of using this algorithm for correcting errors. We use a counting argument to show that for less than $n/2$ errors, where n is the number of processes, the algorithm is able to identify a few number of potential fixes. This demonstrates the usability of the algorithm for debugging these types of communication errors.

This algorithm is a part of the Millipede debugging system [4] we are developing at the University of British Columbia. One tool of interest is a communication debugger that can extract the undelivered messages (and in some cases delivered messages) in the system and suggest corrective measures after the system has deadlocked.

2 Description of Problem

PVM and MPI are two widely used message passing systems which are used in parallel and cluster computing. The basic send and receive calls in PVM and MPI are as follows:

$$\textbf{send}\textit{(buffer, receiver\_nodeID, tag)}$$
$$\textbf{recv}\textit{(buffer, sender\_nodeID, tag)}$$

Mistyping the nodeID or tag value results in a message that is either undelivered or a message received by the wrong process.

For example, consider the simple case of a single error as shown in fig. 1.

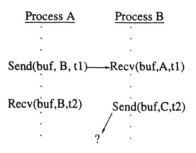

Fig. 1. Simple error.

There is an error in the send call of process B in Fig. 1, B attempts to send a message to A but incorrectly sends it to C. Depending on whether the communication is synchronous or asynchronous process B either blocks, eventually hanging the system or terminates, but in either case it results in an undelivered message in the system. Millipede records a message history and makes it possible to extract both undelivered messages and recently delivered messages from the system. The same kind of error can occur if a tag value is incorrect.

3 The algorithm

Definition 1: Let $\mathcal{S} = (s_0, s_1, \ldots, s_{n-1})$ be an ordered list of senders where each $s_i = (a, b)$ and a, b integer process identifiers (ranks in MPI). Let $\mathcal{R} = (r_0, r_1, \ldots, r_{n-1})$ be an ordered list of receivers where each $r_i = (a, b)$ and again a, b are process identifiers. For $s_i = (a, b) \in \mathcal{S}$, a is fixed by the ID of the sending process, and for $r_i = (a, b) \in \mathcal{R}$, b is fixed by the receiver.

Definition 2: A *match* between a sender $s_i = (a_i, b_i)$ and a receiver $r_j = (a_j, b_j)$ occurs when $(a_i = a_j) \wedge (b_i = b_j)$. The opposite is called a *mismatch*.

For the sake of simplicity we do not consider message tags or wild cards in this first analysis. We will however return to these cases later.

The intuition behind the algorithm is as follows:

Find a permutation of $\mathcal{S}$ denoted π_s and a permutation of $\mathcal{R}$ denoted π_r, where the number of fields that need to be changed in order to obtain a system without any unmatched sends/receives is minimal.

If π_s and π_r are such permutations it follows that after changing the required fields that for all $s_i \in \pi_s$ and $r_j \in \pi_r$ where $(i = j)$ that $a_i = a_j$ and $b_i = b_j$, which means that if the user changes his/her program accordingly the deadlock will disappear.

The desired permutations can be obtained by computing a hamming distance between all possible combinations of permutations of senders and receivers, and choosing the one or ones that give rise to the smallest hamming distance.

Unfortunately this algorithm has time complexity O(n!).

However, it is possible to reduce the problem to a bipartite matching problem [5]. The approach is as follows:

Let $\bar{G} = (\bar{V}, \bar{E})$ be a graph where

- $\bar{V} = \bar{V}_s \cup \bar{V}_r$ where $\bar{V}_s$ and $\bar{V}_r$ both are sets representing all the process ids in the system. ($\bar{V}_s$ represents sending processes and $\bar{V}_r$ represents receiving processes).

- $\bar{E}$ is constructed in the following way.
    - For all messages m not delivered (left in message queues) do the following:
        * If $m = (s, r)$ is an outstanding send add edge (s, r) where $s \in \bar{V}_s$ and $r \in \bar{V}_r$ to $\bar{E}$ with capacity 2.
        * If $m = (r, s)$ is an outstanding receive add edge (r, s) where $s \in \bar{V}_s$ and $r \in \bar{V}_r$ to $\bar{E}$ with capacity 2.
    - Iterate backwards through all successfully delivered messages (u, v) and add edges (u, v) and (v, u) with capacity 2 to $\bar{E}$ **if** no other edge exist in $\bar{E}$ that has u or v as either source or destination.
    - Add edges with capacity 1 to $\bar{E}$ to make $\bar{G}$ a complete graph bipartite graph.

Now run the maximum bipartite graph matching algorithm, which uses flow-graphs to obtain a matching in $\bar{G}$ [?].
This matching results in a system without deadlocks. Furthermore this matching can be obtained by changing a minimum number of fields in the senders and receivers.
The time complexity is $O(|\bar{E}| \cdot |f^*|)$ where $|f^*|$ is the size of the matching. Since $\bar{G}$ is a complete graph $|\bar{E}| = n^2$ and $|f^*| = n$. Therefore the time complexity is $O(n^3)$.
We do not yet have a polynomial time algorithm for the case where tags are considered, but we believe that the bipartite graph matching problem can be adapted to cover this case as well.

4 Algorithm accuracy

In this section we will evaluate the quality of the algorithm, i.e. we will validate that the algorithm does not frequently return an incorrect answer or more than one answer (There could me more than one way to fix a deadlock with a minimum number of field changes). To do this we need to introduce a model that precisely describes a system of senders and receivers equivalent to the one used in the previous section.

In the following n denotes the number of senders and receivers, and k the number of errors in the system. We start out by defining a few concepts.

A *communication configuration* $\mathcal{C}$ is a pair $(\mathcal{S}, \mathcal{R})$ ($\mathcal{S}$ and $\mathcal{R}$ defined in definition 1). SR(n) is a set of all communication configurations with n senders and n receivers.

A send $s_i = (a_i, b_i)$ is called *unmatched* if for $r_{b_i} = (a_j, b_j)$, $a_j \neq a_i$. Equivalently a receive $r_j = (a_j, b_j)$ is called *unmatched* if for $s_{a_j} = (a_i, b_i)$, $b_i \neq b_j$ We call a communication configuration *valid* if it has no unmatched sends or receives.

Given a configuration $(\mathcal{S}, \mathcal{R}) = (\{s_0, \ldots, s_{n-1}\}, \{r_0, \ldots, r_{n-1}\})$ in SR(n), $s_i = (a_i, b_i)$ and $r_j = (a_j, b_j)$. The associated *directed bipartite graph* $G = (V, E)$ is defined by

$$V = \left(\bigcup_{s_i \in \mathcal{S}} a_i \ \cup \ \bigcup_{r_j \in \mathcal{R}} a_j \right)$$

$$E = \left(\bigcup_{s_i \in \mathcal{S}} (a_i, b_i) \right) \ \cup \ \left(\bigcup_{r_j \in \mathcal{R}} (b_j, a_j) \right)$$

Figure 2 shows for a system with two senders and two receivers (SR(2)) the only two valid configurations.

A valid communication configuration $v \in$ SR(n) where $s_i = r_i \ \forall\, i,\ 0 \leq i < n$ is called the *correct* configuration (There is only one correct configuration in SR(n)).

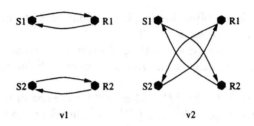

Fig. 2. All valid communication configurations in SR(2).

In Fig. 2 the communication configuration v_1 is the correct communication configuration of SR(2).

From now on the correct configuration will be denoted v_c.

Definition 3: $\mathcal{B}(v, i)$ is the set of communication configurations that can be created by moving i or less arcs from v, $\bar{\mathcal{B}}(v, i) = \mathcal{B}(v, i) \setminus \mathcal{B}(v, i - 1)$ and $\bar{\mathcal{B}}(v, 0) = \mathcal{B}(v, 0) = \{v\}$

Figure 3 shows $\bar{\mathcal{B}}(v_1, 1)$ for v_1 from Fig. 2.

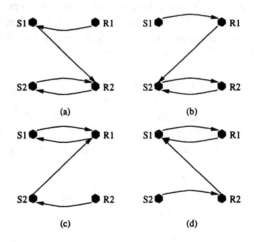

Fig. 3. $\bar{\mathcal{B}}(v_1, 1) \subset$ SR(2).

Given any invalid communication configuration v. In Fig. 4 the boldface $\times$ marks v. The boxes mark valid configurations and the rest, marked by $\times$, are other invalid configurations. The solid line marks $\mathcal{B}(v, 0)$, the dashed line $\mathcal{B}(v, 1)$ and the dotted line $\mathcal{B}(v, 2)$. We wish to correct the invalid communication configuration to be a valid communication configuration by moving as few arrows as possible. This is equivalent to choosing the correct configuration(s) with the smallest hamming distance to v and correcting the fields that do not match. This is done by

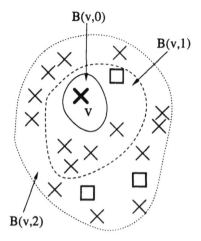

Fig. 4. Example of increasing $\mathcal{B}$ sets.

choosing the first (one or more) valid communication configuration(s) included in the series $\mathcal{B}(v,1), \mathcal{B}(v,2), \ldots$. In the example in Fig. 4 a valid configuration is found in $\mathcal{B}(v,1)$.

We will show that for any invalid communication configuration in $\mathsf{SR}(n)$ the probability that the first encountered valid communication configuration is the correct communication configuration is high. In other words if we introduce k errors into a valid communication configuration $\mathcal{C}$ then the algorithm will in most cases end up proposing $\mathcal{C}$ as the correct way to fix the erroneous system. Only in few cases will it suggest any of the other valid communication configurations in the corresponding system.

Given $\mathsf{SR}(n)$ and a list of the valid configurations $\mathcal{V} = \{v_0, \ldots, v_{n!-1}\}$. Let $k \leq \frac{n}{2}$ be the number of errors in the system. We need to consider the configurations obtainable by introducing one error to all v_i. This is a set of sets:

$$\mathcal{B}_1 = \{\mathcal{B}(v_0, 1), \mathcal{B}(v_1, 1), \ldots, \mathcal{B}(v_{n!-1}, 1)\}$$

If we know for every system with one error that

$$\bigcap_{i=0}^{n!-1} \mathcal{B}(v_i, 1) = \bigcap_{b \in \mathcal{B}_1} b = \emptyset$$

the algorithm will always suggest a correct solution. Figure 5 illustrates this example.

The goal is therefore to show the following:

$$\frac{|B_i \cap B_j|}{|B_i|} \quad \text{and} \quad \frac{|B_i \cap B_j|}{|B_j|} \quad \text{is small} \qquad \forall\, e \leq k, \forall\, B_i, B_j \in \mathcal{B}_e \ , \ (i \neq j).$$

In other words small means an acceptable low fraction of wrongly proposed fixes.

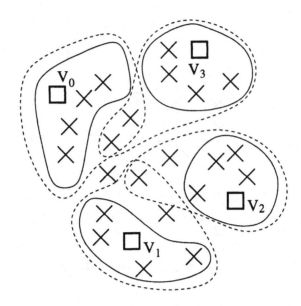

Fig. 5. Example of overlapping $\mathcal{B}$ sets: $\cap_i \mathcal{B}(v_i, 1) = \emptyset$ but $\cap_i \mathcal{B}(v_i, 2) \neq \emptyset$

We will see that this is equivalent to showing that

$$\frac{|B_0 \cap B_i|}{|B_0|} \quad \text{is small} \quad \forall\, e \leq k, \forall\, B_i \in \{\mathcal{B}(v_1, e), \ldots, \mathcal{B}(v_{n!-1}, e)\} \tag{1}$$

where $B_0 = \mathcal{B}(v_c, e)$ where $v_0 = v_c$ is the correct communication configuration of $SR(n)$.

To easier handle these communication configurations we are going to introduce a short hand notation. For each communication configuration in $SR(n)$ (the size of $SR(n)$ is n^{2n}) we assign a $2n$ digit number $s_1 r_1 \ldots s_n r_n$ ($s_i, r_i \in \{0, \ldots, n-1\}$) in the following way:

s_i equals the number of the receiver that sender number i is sending to, and r_i equals the number of the sender that receiver number i is trying to receive from.

For example using the 2 configurations in Fig. 2 as an example we get the following short hand representation: $v_1 = 0011$ and $v_2 = 1100$. Figure 6 shows which configurations can be reached in k steps from the correct configuration.

We now proceed to proving a number of lemmas that will help prove (1).

Lemma 1: The number of valid configurations in $SR(n)$ is $n!$.

Proof: For a configuration to be valid each sender must send to a distinct receiver, and this receiver must receive from this sender. If $s_i = j$ then $r_j = i$. It is therefor sufficient to determine the number of different ways to order n senders. There are $n!$ such ways. □

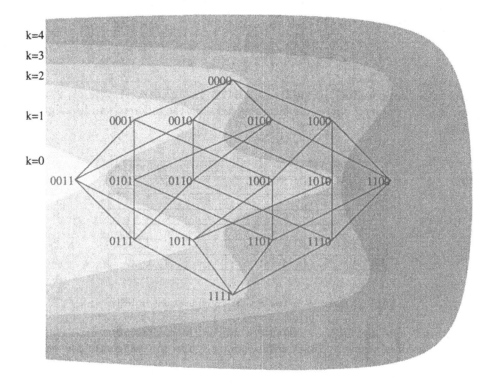

Fig. 6. Configurations that can be reached in k steps from the configuration 0011.

Lemma 2: The size of $\mathcal{B}(v,i)$ denoted $|\mathcal{B}(v,i)|$ is

$$\sum_{j=0}^{i} \binom{2n}{j} (n-1)^j$$

Proof:

$$|\mathcal{B}(v,i)| = |\bigcup_{j=0}^{i} \bar{\mathcal{B}}(v,j)| = \sum_{j=0}^{i} |\bar{\mathcal{B}}(v,j)| = \sum_{j=0}^{i} \binom{2n}{j} (n-1)^j$$

$\square$

Definition 4:

The *distance* between two valid configurations in $\mathsf{SR}(n)$, denoted $d(v_i, v_j)$, is defined as:

$$d(v_i, v_j) = \sum_{l=0}^{2n} [v_{i_l} \neq v_{j_l}]$$

where $v_i = v_{i_1} v_{i_2} \ldots v_{i_{2n}}$, $v_j = v_{j_1} v_{j_2} \ldots v_{j_{2n}}$ and

$$[v_{i_l} \neq v_{j_l}] = \begin{cases} 0 & : & v_{i_l} = v_{j_l} \\ 1 & : & v_{i_l} \neq v_{j_l} \end{cases}$$

The valid configurations in SR(3) are 001122, 110022, 002211, 220011, 221100 and 210210. Figure 7 shows the distances between the different valid configurations.

	001122	110022	002211	122001	221100	210210
001122	0	4	4	6	4	6
110022	4	0	6	4	6	4
002211	4	6	0	4	6	4
122001	6	4	4	0	4	6
221100	4	6	6	4	0	4
210210	6	4	4	6	4	0

Fig. 7. Distances between valid configurations in SR(n).

Lemma 3: For any SR(n), a distance k. and a valid configuration v the number of *valid* configurations in SR(n) with distance k does not depend on the choice of v.

Proof: Permutations are automorphisms. □

Lemma 4: The possible distances between valid configurations in SR(n) are $4, 6, \ldots, 2n - 2, 2n$.

Proof: A necessary condition for a configuration to be valid is that $\{s_1, \ldots, s_n\} = \{r_1, \ldots, r_n\} = \{0, \ldots, n - 1\}$. Since all valid configurations are equivalent consider $v_c = s_1 r_2 s_2 r_2, \ldots, s_n r_n$. A minimum of two send/receive pairs must be switched to obtain a difference valid configuration. This gives a minimum distance of 4. Now choose two send/receive pairs a, b to switch, There are three cases to consider:

1. Both pairs are of the form $s_i r_i = ii$, which means that either they have not been switched before or that they have been switched back to their original state. When these pairs are switched the distance increases by 4.
2. One of the pairs, say a is of the form $s_i r_i = ii$, and the other one (b) is not. When a and b are switched a will contribute with distance 2 to the total distance and b already contributed with distance 2, so the total distance increases by 2.
3. Neither a nor b are of the form $s_i r_i = ii$. Neither will contribute further to the total distance by being switched.

□

Let $\mathcal{D}(v, k)$ be the set of valid configurations with exactly distance k from the valid configuration v.

Lemma 5: The size of $\mathcal{D}(v, m)$ for $m = 2k$ is

$$| \mathcal{D}(v, 2k) | = \binom{n}{k} c_k$$

where

$$c_0 = 1 \quad , \quad c_1 = 0 \quad , \quad c_k = k! - \sum_{i=1}^{k} \binom{k}{i} c_{k-i}$$

Proof: Let v_c be given. The number of valid configurations at distance 0 from v_c is 1 (only v_c itself is distance 0 away!), therefore $c_0 = 1$. According to Lemma 3 no valid configuration is distance 2 away, so $c_1 = 0$. For distance 4 choose two of the n send/receives to move, this can be done in $\binom{n}{2}$ ways. The number of ways these two send/receives can be permuted is 2!, but we must subtract the permutation that does not change anything (and results in v_c), i.e. 1, so we get $\binom{n}{2}(2! - 1) = \binom{n}{2}(2! - \binom{2}{1}c_1 - \binom{2}{2}c_0)$. Set c_2 equal to this expression which is the number of configurations with exactly two permuted send/receives giving distance 4. In general we must subtract the number of configurations that are at the wrong distance. For each distance $m = 2k$ there are $\binom{n}{k}k!$ permutations, and again we must subtract all the permutations that do not exactly permute k send/receives, i.e. give the correct distance of $2k$, so we get:

$$| \mathcal{D}(v, m) | = \binom{n}{k}(k! - \binom{k}{1}c_{k-1} - \binom{k}{2}c_{k-2} \cdots - \binom{k}{k-1}c_1 - \binom{k}{k}c_0) = \binom{n}{k}c_k$$

where

$$c_k = k! - \sum_{i=1}^{k} \binom{k}{i} c_{k-i}$$

$\square$

Consider the following two configurations: $v_1 = 001122$ and $v_2 = 002211$. These two configurations differ in the last four positions, thus have a distance of 4. To computer the intersection $\mathcal{B}(v_1, 2) \cap \mathcal{B}(v_2, 2)$ we must find the configurations that can be reached from both v_1 and v_2 by changing at most 2 positions in each. Since the distance between the two configurations is 4 and we may change at most 2 positions in each configuration, it follows that we must change exactly 2 in each. Choose 2 fields in v_1, say v_{1_i} and v_{1_j}. Change these two positions to have the values of v_{2_i} and v_{2_j} and obtain v_1'. We know that $d(v_1', v2) = 2$. Now change the 2 positions in v_2 that differ from v_1', say v_{2_l} and v_{2_m} to have the values of $v_{1_l} = v_{1_l}'$ and $v_{1_m} = v_{1_m}'$ and obtain v_2'. We now know that $d(v_1', v_2') = 0$. The original distance was 4 and we must change 2 fields in each configuration. The the number of different ways this can be done is $\binom{4}{2} = 6$.

The six configurations that can be obtained are:

$$113\underline{3}\overline{3}\overline{3}, \quad 11\overline{2}\overline{2}\underline{2}\underline{2}, \quad 11\overline{2}\underline{3}2\overline{3}, \quad 113\underline{3}2\overline{3}\overline{3}, \quad 113\underline{3}2\overline{3}2, \quad 11\overline{2}\underline{3}\overline{3}2.$$

The underlined positions are the fields changed in v_1 and the overlined fields are the ones changed in v_2.

According to Lemma 5 all valid configurations are equivalent. Therefore we can simply study the properties of the correct valid configuration v_c of $SR(n)$. We will now determine the number of elements in the intersections of the B sets.

Theorem 1: Let e be the number of errors in a communication system. The number of configurations with e errors for which the algorithm will either suggest a wrong valid configuration or a set of valid configurations where the correct one is included is

$$\left| \bigcup_{v \in \mathcal{V}} B(v_c, e) \cap B(v, e) \right| \leq \sum_{i=2}^{e} \binom{n}{i} c_i \sum_{b=0}^{e} \sum_{a=max\{b, e-b\}}^{e} \sum_{c_o=0}^{min\{\frac{a+b+2i}{2}, 2i-a\}} \mathcal{O}(i, a, b, c_o)$$

where

$$\mathcal{O}(i, a, b, c_o) = [c_{xy} \geq 0 \wedge c_x \geq 0 \wedge c_y \geq 0] \binom{2i}{c_x} \binom{2i - c_x}{c_y} (n-2)^{c_{xy}} \binom{2(n-i)}{c_o} (n-1)^{c_o}$$

and

$$c_{xy} = (a - c_o) + (b - c_o) - 2i$$
$$c_x = 2i - a + c_o$$
$$c_y = 2i - b + c_o$$

Proof: Remember that

$$B(v_c, e) = \bigcup_{a=0}^{e} \bar{B}(v_c, a) \quad \text{and} \quad B(v_j, e) = \bigcup_{b=0}^{e} \bar{B}(v_j, b).$$

For a configuration $v \in B(v_c, a) \cap B(v_j, b)$ with $b = d(v_j, v)$ and $a = d(v_c, v)$ if $a < b$ then v_c will be reported as the correct communication configuration. Since we are concerned with counting the valid communication configurations that are incorrect fixes we only consider cases where $a \geq b$. Additionally, if $a + b < e$ then the intersection between $B(v_c, a)$ and $B(v_j, b)$ is empty. These 3 observations combined yield

$$\left| \bigcup_{v \in \mathcal{V}} B(v_c, e) \cap B(v_i, e) \right| = \left| \bigcup_{i \in \{4, \ldots, 2e\}} \bigcup_{v_j \in \mathcal{D}(v_c, i)} B(v_c, e) \cap B(v_j, e) \right|$$

$$= \sum_{i=2}^{e} \sum_{v_j \in \mathcal{D}(v_c, 2i)} \left| \bigcup_{b=0}^{e} \bigcup_{a=max\{b, e-b\}}^{e} \bar{B}(v_c, a) \cap \bar{B}(v_j, b) \right| \quad (2)$$

We now calculate the value of

$$\left|\bar{B}(v_c, a) \cap \bar{B}(v_j, b)\right|$$

for values a and b where $j = 2i$. Let $x = v_c = x_1 x_2 \ldots x_{2n}$ and $y = v_j = y_1 y_2 \ldots y_{2n}$ with $d(x, y) = j = 2i$. We want to find configurations $z = v = z_1 z_2 \ldots z_{2n}$ such that $d(x, z) = a$ and $d(y, z) = b$. WLOG assume that $x_k = y_k$ for $j + 1 \le k \le 2n$.

$$\overbrace{}^{j} \qquad \overbrace{\phantom{x_{j+1} \cdots x_{2n}}}^{2n-j}$$

$x_1\ x_2\ \cdots\ x_j$	$x_{j+1}\ \cdots\ x_{2n}$
$z_1\ z_2\ \cdots\ z_j$	$z_{j+1}\ \cdots\ z_{2n}$
$y_1\ y_2\ \cdots\ y_j$	$y_{j+1}\ \cdots\ y_{2n}$

Now define

$$C_y = \{z_k : 1 \le k \le j : z_k = x_k \wedge z_k \ne y_k\}$$
$$C_x = \{z_k : 1 \le k \le j : z_k \ne x_k \wedge z_k = y_k\}$$
$$C_{xy} = \{z_k : 1 \le k \le j : z_k \ne x_k \wedge z_k \ne y_k\}$$
$$C_o = \{z_k : j + 1 \le k \le 2n : z_k \ne x_k \wedge z_k \ne y_k\}$$
$$c_x = |C_x|$$
$$c_y = |C_y|$$
$$c_{xy} = |C_{xy}|$$
$$c_o = |C_o|$$

A z-configuration must satisfy

$$\binom{a}{b} = c_{xy}\binom{1}{1} + c_x\binom{1}{0} + c_y\binom{0}{1} + c_o\binom{1}{1}$$

since $d(x, z) = a$ and $d(y, z) = b$.

This gives us the following 3 equations.

$$a = c_{xy} + c_y + c_o$$
$$b = c_{xy} + c_x + c_o \qquad (3)$$
$$j = c_{xy} + c_x + c_y$$

The last equation follows from the fact that $x_k \ne y_k$ for $1 \le k \le j$.
If we solve with $a' = a - c_o$ and $b' = b - c_o$ we get the following matrix equation:

$$\begin{pmatrix} 1 & 0 & 1 \\ 1 & 1 & 0 \\ 1 & 1 & 1 \end{pmatrix} \begin{pmatrix} c_{xy} \\ c_x \\ c_y \end{pmatrix} = \begin{pmatrix} a' \\ b' \\ j \end{pmatrix}$$

By inverting the matrix we can compute values for c_{xy}, c_x, and c_y:

$$\begin{pmatrix} c_{xy} \\ c_x \\ c_y \end{pmatrix} = \begin{pmatrix} 1 & 1 & -1 \\ -1 & 0 & 1 \\ 0 & -1 & 1 \end{pmatrix} \begin{pmatrix} a' \\ b' \\ j \end{pmatrix} = \begin{pmatrix} a' + b' - j \\ j - a' \\ j - b' \end{pmatrix} = \begin{pmatrix} a + b - j - 2c_o \\ j - a + c_o \\ j - b + c_o \end{pmatrix}$$

where the number of fields where z differs from x but not from y is c_x, the number of fields where z differs from y but not x is c_y, and the number of fields where z differs from both x and y is c_{xy}. We now look at the different ways of choosing fields in z that satisfy these constraints. Of the j fields where $x_k \neq y_k$ we must choose c_x where z differs from x but not y. Of the remaining $(j - c_x)$ we must choose c_y fields. The rest of the c_{xy} fields are pre-chosen. Of the $(2n - j)$ fields where x and y do not differ we must choose c_o fields where z differs.

The values of the C_x and C_y fields are chosen to be the values of the opposite string, i.e. for the c_x chosen fields the value is that of y and vice versa for the c_y chosen ones. The remaining C_{xy} fields can take any value except those of the corresponding fields in x and y, so that leaves $(n - 2)$ choices for these c_{xy} fields. The C_o fields can take any value except that of the corresponding fields of x and y (which are the same!), i.e. there are $(n - 1)$ different choices for these values.

By substituting these values in equation (2) and summing over all valid values of c_o (i.e. values for c_o that produce non-negative values for c_{xy}, c_x and c_y) we get the number of configurations with distance a to x and distance b to y. The Iverson function $[c_x \geq 0 \wedge c_y \geq 0 \wedge c_{xy} \geq 0]$ assures valid values of c_{xy}, c_x and c_y. Taking into consideration that $c_o \leq \frac{a+b+2i}{2}$ and $c_o \leq 2i - a$ (See equation (3)) we arrive at

$$\sum_{i=2}^{e} |\mathcal{D}(v_c, 2i)| \sum_{b=0}^{e} \sum_{a=max\{b,e-b\}}^{e} \sum_{c_o=0}^{min\{\frac{a+b+2i}{2}, 2i-a\}} \mathcal{O}(i, a, b, c_o) =$$

$$\sum_{i=2}^{e} \binom{n}{i} c_i \sum_{b=0}^{e} \sum_{a=max\{b,e-b\}}^{e} \sum_{c_o=0}^{min\{\frac{a+b+2i}{2}, 2i-a\}} \mathcal{O}(i, a, b, c_o) \qquad (4)$$

where c_i are the constants from Lemma 4, and

$$\mathcal{O}(i, a, b, c_o) = [c_{xy} \geq 0][c_x \geq 0][c_y \geq 0] \binom{2i}{c_x} \binom{2i - c_x}{c_y} (n-2)^{c_{xy}} \binom{2(n - i)}{c_o} (n-1)$$

and c_{xy}, c_x, c_y are given as follows:

$$c_{xy} = (a - c_o) + (b - c_o) - 2i$$
$$c_x = 2i - a + c_o$$
$$c_y = 2i - b + c_o$$

n	Number of errors (e)									
	e = 1		e = 2		e = 3		e = 4		e = 5	
	Wrong	Ambg.	Wrong	Ambg.	Wrong	Ambg.	Wrong	Ambg.	Wrong	Ambg.
2	0.00%	0.00%	0.00%	54.55%						
3	0.00%	0.00%	16.44%	8.22%						
4	0.00%	0.00%	10.83%	2.17%						
5	0.00%	0.00%	7.10%	0.79%	21.40%	1.59%				
6	0.00%	0.00%	4.91%	0.35%	14.83%	0.75%				
7	0.00%	0.00%	3.57%	0.18%	10.79%	0.40%	19.89%	0.26%		
8	0.00%	0.00%	2.70%	0.10%	8.17%	0.23%	13.51%	0.11%		
9	0.00%	0.00%	2.11%	0.06%	6.38%	0.14%	9.54%	0.05%	19.87%	0.04%
10	0.00%	0.00%	1.70%	0.04%	5.12%	0.09%	6.97%	0.03%	13.62%	0.02%

Fig. 8. Failure rate for algorithm - Incorrect fixes and ambiguous fixes.

□

Using equation (4) we can not compute an upper bound for the fraction (1). Figure 8 shows the estimated failure rate for the algorithm. An ambiguous fix is when more than one valid configuration is at the minimum distance.

5 Message tags

We now briefly turn to message passing that includes message tags. We will not formally analyze this case, but briefly argue that the chances of the algorithm being able to predict the correct solution increases proportionally to the number of different message tags used.

Figure 9 is a copy of Fig. 2 where we have introduced message tags. The S_1 and R_1 both send/receive with tag 11, and S_2 and R_2 both send/receive with tag 22. It is obvious that v_2 is no longer a valid configuration as there is a tag mismatch between S_1 and R_2 and between S_2 and R_1. In fact v_2 is now a configuration with at least 2 errors.

By introducing message tags into a communication system, and by choosing them carefully, i.e. in a meaningful way with respect to the message they are associated with, the risks of the algorithm predicting a wrong solution is greatly reduced.

As an example consider SR(2). As seen in the previous example the 54.55% ambiguity rate has disappeared as v_2 is no longer a valid configuration. This holds true if 2 errors are introduced in the sender or receiver ids. The correct valid configuration v_1 is distance 2 away where v_2 is distance 4 away. Similarly if 2 errors are introduced into the tags the correct valid configuration will be distance 2 away where as the wrong valid configuration will be distance 4 away.

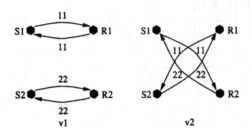

Fig. 9. Introducing message tags.

Using wild cards is another challenging concept. The use of these is mainly for two reasons: dynamic communication or a shortcut for the programmer, i.e. used instead of a known process id. When introducing wild cards into a communication system the degree of freedom with respect to field values increases. This decreases the success rate of an algorithm like the one presented.

6 Conclusion

We have presented an algorithm that proposes changes in deadlocked message passing systems that will correct the communication errors so the deadlock disappears. If a small number of errors occur in an otherwise working message passing system then we can correct these errors with a good probability. By carefully choosing message tags and by associating different tags with different types of communication the risks of wrong sends going through is substantially reduced. Furthermore and also the ability to predict the correct communication configuration is greatly increased.

7 Acknowledgements

We would like to thank Alex Brodsky for always being willing to lend a helping hand, and a special thanks to Bettina Speckman for not only helping with figuring it all out but also for the time she has spent on reading and helping us rewrite this entire paper.

References

1. James Arthur Kohl and G. A. Geist. The PVM 3.4 Tracing Facility and XPVM 1.1. *Proceedings of the 29th Annual Hawaii International Conference on System Sciences*, pages 290–299, 1996.
2. D. Kranzlmüller and J. Volkert. Using Different Levels of Abstraction for Parallel Programming Debugging. In *Proccedings of the 1997 IASTED (International Conference on Intelligent Information)*, pages 523–529, 1997.
3. C. M. Pancake. What Users Need in Parallel Tool Support: Survey Results and Analysis. Technical Report CSTR 94-80-3, Oregon State University, June 1994.
4. Jan Pedersen and Alan Wagner. Sequential Debugging of Parallel Programs. In *Proceedings of the international conference on communications in computing, CIC'2000*. CSREA Press, June 2000.
5. Oliver Pretzel. *Error-Correcting Codes and Finite Fields*. Clarendon Press, 1992.

Lecture Notes in Computer Science

For information about Vols. 1–1935
please contact your bookseller or Springer-Verlag

Vol. 1936: P. Robertson, H. Shrobe, R. Laddaga (Eds.), Self-Adaptive Software. Proceedings, 2000. VIII, 249 pages. 2001.

Vol. 1937: R. Dieng, O. Corby (Eds.), Knowledge Engineering and Knowledge Management. Proceedings, 2000. XIII, 457 pages. 2000. (Subseries LNAI).

Vol. 1938: S. Rao, K.I. Sletta (Eds.), Next Generation Networks. Proceedings, 2000. XI, 392 pages. 2000.

Vol. 1939: A. Evans, S. Kent, B. Selic (Eds.), «UML» – The Unified Modeling Language. Proceedings, 2000. XIV, 572 pages. 2000.

Vol. 1940: M. Valero, K. Joe, M. Kitsuregawa, H. Tanaka (Eds.), High Performance Computing. Proceedings, 2000. XV, 595 pages. 2000.

Vol. 1941: A.K. Chhabra, D. Dori (Eds.), Graphics Recognition. Proceedings, 1999. XI, 346 pages. 2000.

Vol. 1942: H. Yasuda (Ed.), Active Networks. Proceedings, 2000. XI, 424 pages. 2000.

Vol. 1943: F. Koornneef, M. van der Meulen (Eds.), Computer Safety, Reliability and Security. Proceedings, 2000. X, 432 pages. 2000.

Vol. 1944: K.R. Dittrich, G. Guerrini, I. Merlo, M. Oliva, M.E. Rodriguez (Eds.), Objects and Databases. Proceedings, 2000. X, 199 pages. 2001.

Vol. 1945: W. Grieskamp, T. Santen, B. Stoddart (Eds.), Integrated Formal Methods. Proceedings, 2000. X, 441 pages. 2000.

Vol. 1946: P. Palanque, F. Paternò (Eds.), Interactive Systems. Proceedings, 2000. X, 251 pages. 2001.

Vol. 1947: T. Sørevik, F. Manne, R. Moe, A.H. Gebremedhin (Eds.), Applied Parallel Computing. Proceedings, 2000. XII, 400 pages. 2001.

Vol. 1948: T. Tan, Y. Shi, W. Gao (Eds.), Advances in Multimodal Interfaces – ICMI 2000. Proceedings, 2000. XVI, 678 pages. 2000.

Vol. 1949: R. Connor, A. Mendelzon (Eds.), Research Issues in Structured and Semistructured Database Programming. Proceedings, 1999. XII, 325 pages. 2000.

Vol. 1950: D. van Melkebeek, Randomness and Completeness in Computational Complexity. XV, 196 pages. 2000.

Vol. 1951: F. van der Linden (Ed.), Software Architectures for Product Families. Proceedings, 2000. VIII, 255 pages. 2000.

Vol. 1952: M.C. Monard, J. Simão Sichman (Eds.), Advances in Artificial Intelligence. Proceedings, 2000. XV, 498 pages. 2000. (Subseries LNAI).

Vol. 1953: G. Borgefors, I. Nyström, G. Sanniti di Baja (Eds.), Discrete Geometry for Computer Imagery. Proceedings, 2000. XI, 544 pages. 2000.

Vol. 1954: W.A. Hunt, Jr., S.D. Johnson (Eds.), Formal Methods in Computer-Aided Design. Proceedings, 2000. XI, 539 pages. 2000.

Vol. 1955: M. Parigot, A. Voronkov (Eds.), Logic for Programming and Automated Reasoning. Proceedings, 2000. XIII, 487 pages. 2000. (Subseries LNAI).

Vol. 1956: T. Coquand, P. Dybjer, B. Nordström, J. Smith (Eds.), Types for Proofs and Programs. Proceedings, 1999. VII, 195 pages. 2000.

Vol. 1957: P. Ciancarini, M. Wooldridge (Eds.), Agent-Oriented Software Engineering. Proceedings, 2000. X, 323 pages. 2001.

Vol. 1960: A. Ambler, S.B. Calo, G. Kar (Eds.), Services Management in Intelligent Networks. Proceedings, 2000. X, 259 pages. 2000.

Vol. 1961: J. He, M. Sato (Eds.), Advances in Computing Science – ASIAN 2000. Proceedings, 2000. X, 299 pages. 2000.

Vol. 1963: V. Hlaváč, K.G. Jeffery, J. Wiedermann (Eds.), SOFSEM 2000: Theory and Practice of Informatics. Proceedings, 2000. XI, 460 pages. 2000.

Vol. 1964: J. Malenfant, S. Moisan, A. Moreira (Eds.), Object-Oriented Technology. Proceedings, 2000. XI, 309 pages. 2000.

Vol. 1965: Ç. K. Koç, C. Paar (Eds.), Cryptographic Hardware and Embedded Systems – CHES 2000. Proceedings, 2000. XI, 355 pages. 2000.

Vol. 1966: S. Bhalla (Ed.), Databases in Networked Information Systems. Proceedings, 2000. VIII, 247 pages. 2000.

Vol. 1967: S. Arikawa, S. Morishita (Eds.), Discovery Science. Proceedings, 2000. XII, 332 pages. 2000. (Subseries LNAI).

Vol. 1968: H. Arimura, S. Jain, A. Sharma (Eds.), Algorithmic Learning Theory. Proceedings, 2000. XI, 335 pages. 2000. (Subseries LNAI).

Vol. 1969: D.T. Lee, S.-H. Teng (Eds.), Algorithms and Computation. Proceedings, 2000. XIV, 578 pages. 2000.

Vol. 1970: M. Valero, V.K. Prasanna, S. Vajapeyam (Eds.), High Performance Computing – HiPC 2000. Proceedings, 2000. XVIII, 568 pages. 2000.

Vol. 1971: R. Buyya, M. Baker (Eds.), Grid Computing – GRID 2000. Proceedings, 2000. XIV, 229 pages. 2000.

Vol. 1972: A. Omicini, R. Tolksdorf, F. Zambonelli (Eds.), Engineering Societies in the Agents World. Proceedings, 2000. IX, 143 pages. 2000. (Subseries LNAI).

Vol. 1973: J. Van den Bussche, V. Vianu (Eds.), Database Theory – ICDT 2001. Proceedings, 2001. X, 451 pages. 2001.

Vol. 1974: S. Kapoor, S. Prasad (Eds.), FST TCS 2000: Foundations of Software Technology and Theoretical Computer Science. Proceedings, 2000. XIII, 532 pages. 2000.

Vol. 1975: J. Pieprzyk, E. Okamoto, J. Seberry (Eds.), Information Security. Proceedings, 2000. X, 323 pages. 2000.

Vol. 1976: T. Okamoto (Ed.), Advances in Cryptology – ASIACRYPT 2000. Proceedings, 2000. XII, 630 pages. 2000.

Vol. 1977: B. Roy, E. Okamoto (Eds.), Progress in Cryptology – INDOCRYPT 2000. Proceedings, 2000. X, 295 pages. 2000.

Vol. 1978: B. Schneier (Ed.), Fast Software Encryption. Proceedings, 2000. VIII, 315 pages. 2001.

Vol. 1979: S. Moss, P. Davidsson (Eds.), Multi-Agent-Based Simulation. Proceedings, 2000. VIII, 267 pages. 2001. (Subseries LNAI).

Vol. 1983: K.S. Leung, L.-W. Chan, H. Meng (Eds.), Intelligent Data Engineering and Automated Learning – IDEAL 2000. Proceedings, 2000. XVI, 573 pages. 2000.

Vol. 1984: J. Marks (Ed.), Graph Drawing. Proceedings, 2001. XII, 419 pages. 2001.

Vol. 1985: J. Davidson, S.L. Min (Eds.), Languages, Compilers, and Tools for Embedded Systems. Proceedings, 2000. VIII, 221 pages. 2001.

Vol. 1987: K.-L. Tan, M.J. Franklin, J. C.-S. Lui (Eds.), Mobile Data Management. Proceedings, 2001. XIII, 289 pages. 2001.

Vol. 1988: L. Vulkov, J. Waśniewski, P. Yalamov (Eds.), Numerical Analysis and Its Applications. Proceedings, 2000. XIII, 782 pages. 2001.

Vol. 1989: M. Ajmone Marsan, A. Bianco (Eds.), Quality of Service in Multiservice IP Networks. Proceedings, 2001. XII, 440 pages. 2001.

Vol. 1990: I.V. Ramakrishnan (Ed.), Practical Aspects of Declarative Languages. Proceedings, 2001. VIII, 353 pages. 2001.

Vol. 1991: F. Dignum, C. Sierra (Eds.), Agent Mediated Electronic Commerce. VIII, 241 pages. 2001. (Subseries LNAI).

Vol. 1992: K. Kim (Ed.), Public Key Cryptography. Proceedings, 2001. XI, 423 pages. 2001.

Vol. 1993: E. Zitzler, K. Deb, L. Thiele, C.A.Coello Coello, D. Corne (Eds.), Evolutionary Multi-Criterion Optimization. Proceedings, 2001. XIII, 712 pages. 2001.

Vol. 1995: M. Sloman, J. Lobo, E.C. Lupu (Eds.), Policies for Distributed Systems and Networks. Proceedings, 2001. X, 263 pages. 2001.

Vol. 1997: D. Suciu, G. Vossen (Eds.), The World Wide Web and Databases. Proceedings, 2000. XII, 275 pages. 2001.

Vol. 1998: R. Klette, S. Peleg, G. Sommer (Eds.), Robot Vision. Proceedings, 2001. IX, 285 pages. 2001.

Vol. 1999: W. Emmerich, S. Tai (Eds.), Engineering Distributed Objects. Proceedings, 2000. VIII, 271 pages. 2001.

Vol. 2000: R. Wilhelm (Ed.), Informatics: 10 Years Back, 10 Years Ahead. IX, 369 pages. 2001.

Vol. 2003: F. Dignum, U. Cortés (Eds.), Agent Mediated Electronic Commerce III. XII, 193 pages. 2001. (Subseries LNAI).

Vol. 2004: A. Gelbukh (Ed.), Computational Linguistics and Intelligent Text Processing. Proceedings, 2001. XII, 528 pages. 2001.

Vol. 2006: R. Dunke, A. Abran (Eds.), New Approaches in Software Measurement. Proceedings, 2000. VIII, 245 pages. 2001.

Vol. 2007: J.F. Roddick, K. Hornsby (Eds.), Temporal, Spatial, and Spatio-Temporal Data Mining. Proceedings, 2000. VII, 165 pages. 2001. (Subseries LNAI).

Vol. 2009: H. Federrath (Ed.), Designing Privacy Enhancing Technologies. Proceedings, 2000. X, 231 pages. 2001.

Vol. 2010: A. Ferreira, H. Reichel (Eds.), STACS 2001. Proceedings, 2001. XV, 576 pages. 2001.

Vol. 2013: S. Singh, N. Murshed, W. Kropatsch (Eds.), Advances in Pattern Recognition – ICAPR 2001. Proceedings, 2001. XIV, 476 pages. 2001.

Vol. 2015: D. Won (Ed.), Information Security and Cryptology – ICISC 2000. Proceedings, 2000. X, 261 pages. 2001.

Vol. 2018: M. Pollefeys, L. Van Gool, A. Zisserman, A. Fitzgibbon (Eds.), 3D Structure from Images – SMILE 2000. Proceedings, 2000. X, 243 pages. 2001.

Vol. 2020: D. Naccache (Ed.), Topics in Cryptology – CT-RSA 2001. Proceedings, 2001. XII, 473 pages. 2001

Vol. 2021: J. N. Oliveira, P. Zave (Eds.), FME 2001: Formal Methods for Increasing Software Productivity. Proceedings, 2001. XIII, 629 pages. 2001.

Vol. 2024: H. Kuchen, K. Ueda (Eds.), Functional and Logic Programming. Proceedings, 2001. X, 391 pages. 2001.

Vol. 2026: F. Müller (Ed.), High-Level Parallel Programming Models and Supportive Environments. Proceedings, 2001. IX, 137 pages. 2001.

Vol. 2027: R. Wilhelm (Ed.), Compiler Construction. Proceedings, 2001. XI, 371 pages. 2001.

Vol. 2028: D. Sands (Ed.), Programming Languages and Systems. Proceedings, 2001. XIII, 433 pages. 2001.

Vol. 2029: H. Hussmann (Ed.), Fundamental Approaches to Software Engineering. Proceedings, 2001. XIII, 349 pages. 2001.

Vol. 2030: F. Honsell, M. Miculan (Eds.), Foundations of Software Science and Computation Structures. Proceedings, 2001. XII, 413 pages. 2001.

Vol. 2031: T. Margaria, W. Yi (Eds.), Tools and Algorithms for the Construction and Analysis of Systems. Proceedings, 2001. XIV, 588 pages. 2001.

Vol. 2034: M.D. Di Benedetto, A. Sangiovanni-Vincentelli (Eds.), Hybrid Systems: Computation and Control. Proceedings, 2001. XIV, 516 pages. 2001.

Vol. 2035: D. Cheung, G.J. Williams, Q. Li (Eds.), Advances in Knowledge Discovery and Data Mining – PAKDD 2001. Proceedings, 2001. XVIII, 596 pages. 2001. (Subseries LNAI).

Vol. 2038: J. Miller, M. Tomassini, P.L. Lanzi, C. Ryan, A.G.B. Tettamanzi, W.B. Langdon (Eds.), Genetic Programming. Proceedings, 2001. XI, 384 pages. 2001.